Who Rules the World,
God or Satan?

JOHN ABRAHAM

ISBN 978-1-64299-067-6 (paperback)
ISBN 978-1-64299-068-3 (digital)

Copyright © 2018 by John Abraham

All rights reserved. No part of this publication may be reproduced, distributed, or transmitted in any form or by any means, including photocopying, recording, or other electronic or mechanical methods without the prior written permission of the publisher. For permission requests, solicit the publisher via the address below.

Christian Faith Publishing, Inc.
832 Park Avenue
Meadville, PA 16335
www.christianfaithpublishing.com

Printed in the United States of America

CHAPTER 1

The Truth about Satan

This is an unusual but very important question, normally neglected by everyone, including theologians, Bible scholars, all common Christians, and religious leaders of all faith. Can anybody give a direct answer? Like yes or no? It appears to be very hard, and no one wants to even think about it. Well the world exists, and we live in it, and there is a constant conflict between God and Satan, good and evil, moral and immoral, justice and injustice, righteousness and wickedness because in every case both are existing. Most religious faiths agree the existence of heaven (where only God and good exists) and hell (where Satan and evil exists). But mankind (human) does not want to accept these facts simply because their ego does not allow them to accept that they are under bondage or slavery (whatever you want to call it). They want to live free, calling it as liberty and freedom or human rights. In reality, it makes no sense because whether you like it or not, good and evil exist, and we are facing them in our life daily. We are not living in the world devoid of good and evil.

So the answer to the above question could be logically both! But the point here is, how could there be two rulers on the earth simultaneously—God and Satan? Have they got two different kingdoms separately on the same earth or in the same planet? What does it mean when we say heaven (commonly referred to as the *third heaven* in the Scriptures), whose sovereign ruler is God, where there is no place for evil and wickedness, and the mid-heaven (commonly referred to as *second heaven*), where the sole occupancy is by Satan, where he and all evil spirits dwell and occupy, causing all atrocities commonly called as evil on the planet earth, where human beings are living? Is it surprising? But these are facts of the matter and could not be denied at all. The other way to say it is that mankind is in the middle of God and Satan and good and evil. Doesn't it look strange and pathetic?

Everybody is aware of the sufferings and all evil consequences commonly seen all over the world, but nobody is able to give a straight and convincing answer to the question "Who is responsible?" Either God or Satan. Many blame God straight away and easily for everything. Some do not want to blame God because of their faith and fear of God. But no one seems to have the real knowledge and understanding of the real cause. Many others do not want to blame Satan because they think they may not be able to live as they like according to their will and pleasure because blaming Satan is accepting good and hating evil, which would control them from living freely according to what they think is freedom and liberty. Ultimately, we are all living in illusions and not in reality.

> God rules the whole universe including the planet earth, and Satan rules the world systems and the fallen mankind in the earth only.

Because of this kind of situation, there are always conflicts and sufferings. Actually, man asked for it! God did not want or never wanted mankind to suffer at all. When God created everything on the face of the earth, He found them all to be good (Genesis 1), and as humans, when we look around and the entire creations, it looks so good and wonderful, and we can keep admiring them all our life. But alas! Something happened! Everything was lost and went topsy-turvy. When we look at the nature, it clearly spells out the splendor of His creation. Having done all, finally God wanted to create man in His own image and likeness and wanted to put him as the ruler of this earth and everything in it. And He did so. But at the same time, by His foreknowledge, He knew that man is going to fall and lose his dominion and the authority to rule the earth. That is why everyone is asking, "Having known it, why did He do so?" Man lost his power and authority to Satan and became his slave from the day he fell in to sin. The Bible also clearly tells us that sin has separated mankind from God and a veil has been formed between God and mankind and man has lost the privilege of seeing God and any fellowship or communication with Him (Isaiah 59:1). The very nature Cain, the firstborn of Adam and Eve, exhibited hatred toward his own brother and murdered him itself is very convincing evidence that man has become slave to Satan, or the Devil, however you want to call him.

Satan has taken over the rulership over mankind. This can be understood very easily from the narratives given in Genesis in the account of creation of mankind. God created Adam and then Eve and put them in the Garden of Eden. He blessed them to multiply and fill the earth and also gave them dominion over all the rest of His creations. But something else happened. Satan, who was already there, deceived Eve first and, through her, Adam also. By eating the forbidden fruit, they disobeyed God's commandment and sinned against God. Because of the sin, they lost the dominion over themselves and also over everything, and they became slave to Satan. Satan has taken over the rulership over mankind. The first thing they lost was the direct communication with their creator, God the Father. Satan was able to maintain his communication with men.

The Scriptures say in Isaiah 59:1, your sins have separated you from God. The same sin has taken you in to slavery under Satan. Satan was destined to die, and he brought the same curse of death to mankind. Death simply means separation. There are two kind of death referred in the scriptures. One is *spiritual death*, and the other is *physical death*. Spiritual death means *separation from God*. Physical death means our soul and spirit getting separated from our physical body. Satan was already spiritually dead. He is waiting for his physical death until *second death* (Revelation 20:14). We will learn more about second death in the last chapter of this book. Mankind also is spiritually dead (separated from God since birth), and they die physically when their soul and spirit leaves their body. Later, everyone is going to face judgment, when his eternal destiny will be determined by our Lord Jesus Christ.

Men are not able to see God or communicate with Him because we are under the bondage of Satan since our birth into this world. In order to get back to the original state of how Adam and Eve was with God, we have to be delivered from the bondage of Satan. Every human being is under the curse of death, which came upon them because of Satan. He is a murderer and a liar from the beginning (John 8:44). We also read in the scriptures that we are Satan's children and he is our father. There can be no truth in him. Jesus Himself said, "You do not hear the words of God because you are not of God" (John 8:47).

Then what happened from God's side? What about the rest of all the creations of God? They are all still under direct rulership of God, which was very clearly indicated by Jesus Christ Himself in the following passage: Matthew 6:25–34. Look at the birds of the skies. They neither sow nor reap. But the Father in heaven is providing everything for them. None of them suffer for anything. The Father in heaven takes care of them. None of the living creatures have conscience except the human beings. He told Adam that you have to toil on the earth for your own living. He also told men to learn to trust God for all needs and provisions. And you will not get anything unless you ask (Matthew 7:7). Your Father in heaven knows all your needs. Unless you ask believing on Him you are not going to receive anything from Him. Otherwise, you have to take care of yourself. All of His other creations according to the scriptures only praise God every day for their provisions except man. Read Matthew 6:32. Your heavenly Father knows that you have need of all these things. But only when you seek the kingdom of God first and His righteousness, then all these things shall be added unto you (Matthew 6:33). The lives of all living creatures other than mankind are subjected to death to be made available for food for mankind. They neither sinned nor ate the fruit from the tree of knowledge for knowing good and evil. Satan cannot influence them; neither do men.

Obviously the entire universe is ruled by God. Satan has no access or control over any other part of the universe, including the nature; neither will they obey his commands or directions. God calls the stars by name and put them all in their proper positions, and they just exist for billions of years and will exist into timeless eternity unless otherwise God Himself changes His mind, will, and plans. We do not know about it, and He has hidden it from the understanding of mankind or the so-called scientists.

God has absolute control over nature and the environment surrounding the earth. Jesus, when He was on the face of this earth, He exercised and exhibited His power and authority over nature at more than one occasions. The flood in the days of Noah (Genesis 6), the dividing of the Red Sea (Exodus 14), the dividing of the Jordan River (Joshua 3), the falling of fire from the heaven in the days of Elijah (1 Kings 18), the miracle of deliverance from the fiery furnace in the days of Shadrach, Meshach, and Abednego (Daniel 3), the miracle the whale swallowing Jonah (Jonah 1–2), etc. confirm God's absolute power and authority over nature. Could Satan at any time exercise any authority over nature? Not at all! He can interfere into nature only when God permits him.

Evidences That Satan Is Ruling the World Systems and the Fallen Mankind

Satan has a kingdom on the earth. At the very first instant when the devil (Satan) encountered Jesus to tempt Him, he showed Him all the kingdoms of the world and said, "All the power and glory of them is *delivered* unto me, and whomsoever I will, I give it to them" (Luke 4:5–6). Jesus did not dispute his authority over the world and the kingdoms of the world. He works through princes like Beelzebub. The scribes once accused Jesus that He was casting out demons by the prince of the devils. But Jesus refuted by saying, "If I do so, how could that kingdom stand? Will the devil cast out the members of its own kingdom?" Mark 3:22–26.

Satan is ruler of part-terrestrial and part-celestial realms. He is occupying the second heaven in the celestial realm and rules the world as well. Paul writes to Ephesians (2:2) that you were once walked to the course of this world and according to the prince of the power of the air, the spirit which now works in the children of disobedience.

He is confirming it in Ephesians 6:10–18. Jesus confirms it in John 12:31. Paul further goes on to say in 2 Corinthians 4:4, referring to Satan that he is the god of this world.

Satan rules the world systems. He has full control over businesses, social, political, and religious activities of the majority of mankind, save the true believers and true Christians who follow the Lord faithfully. When Jesus was questioned about the tribute (tax) to be paid, Jesus answered them, saying, "Pay to Caesar which belongs to him and the Lord which belongs to Him" (Mark 12:17).

Satan rules the world by his subjects, which are fallen angels, fallen men and women, and demons of various kinds (Matthew 25:41, Revelation 12:7–12, John 8:44, 1 John 3:8–10, James 2:19).

Satan is the head of some religions and is the leader of many religious affairs. Many religious heads or leaders are totally under his rulership and are controlled by him. He turns them all against the true and only God, the God of the Bible (2 Corinthians 11:14; Revelations 2:9, 3:9).

Some of Satan's Privileges and Powers

- He is a spiritual being (angel like) with a spiritual body (not of flesh and blood), soul, and spirit (Ezekiel 28:11–17, Revelation 12:1–12).
- He can go from place to place because he is a Spirit unlike anyone else who are in the human form and in the flesh (Job 1:1–6, 2:1–7; Matthew 4:10–11; Mark 4:15).
- He has access to enter heaven (Job 1:16, 2:1–7).
- He is the deceiver of all men (2 Corinthians 11:14, Revelation 12:9, 20:1–10).
- He is the leader of all sinners (unbelievers) and backsliders, all who deny God, and the Savior Jesus Christ, all the ungodly, unrighteous of the whole human race (1 John 3:8–10, 1 Timothy 5:15), and all spirit rebels (Matthew 9:34, Ephesians 6:10–18).
- He causes all sicknesses, disease, physical and mental maladies in the human beings (Luke 13:16, Acts 10:38).

- He hinders answer to prayers from reaching the people who had prayed (Daniel 10:12–21).
- He is a liar and father of all lies and a murderer from the beginning (John 8:44).
- He is completely and totally wicked. He is an embodiment of wickedness (Matthew 13:18, 1 John 3:8, 5:18)
- He can perform pseudo miracles to deceive people through magic, sorcery, etc. (Acts 8:9–20, 2 Thessalonians 2:9).
- He can bring lawlessness through world systems. The political, social, and the religious systems are under his control.
- He can oppress and possess men (Matthew 4:24, 7:22, 8:16).
- He can afflict men and women with sickness and bondage (Luke 13:11–13, Matthew 8:16–17).
- He is unclean (Mark 3:11, 5:2–13, 6:7, 7:25).

I have listed only a few here, and there is a lot more.

The Works or Activities of Satan

In general, his work is to oppose God whenever and wherever possible. For this reason, his work varies in many respects with the purpose of God in different dispensations and ages. During the Old Testament times, his great work was to cause the fall on man, usurp man's dominion, and try to prevent the coming of the Messiah into this world in order to avert his own defeat and pending doom. He even tried to deceive Jesus through the temptations to give up His dominion and the purpose of His coming. He did not want Jesus to go to the cross and die the atoning death by several means, but Jesus overcame all of them. Now he is cut down to his size and is waiting for his total condemnation into the lake of fire after the great white throne judgment.

The main seat of his attack on human beings is their *mind*. There is an old saying as follows: "An idle mind is the devil's workshop." But even an active mind could fall in to his deceptions. Both are dangerous. An alert mind to understand the wiles of the devil, to judge between good and evil, with an attitude to fear God and shun evil, is very important. Man has been given the freewill as well as Satan was. It could be used in many ways. Humans are moral beings, unlike animals. Morality differentiates man from the animals. The devil knows this very well. God is the moral law giver. Devil (Satan) is the source of lawlessness. Man is a moral being. Morality is the greatest and highest attribute of God, and God expects that same character from mankind. Satan's character is just the opposite. He hates morality mainly because it pleases God. Immorality leads to lawlessness and uncleanness. That is why he likes it, and that is what he wants—to fill man's thoughts with these things. By saturating man's thoughts with these ideas, he is able to exercise complete control over mankind. Thus, mankind has become slaves to Satan and is totally under his bondage. This is what the Bible describes as "all have sinned and come short of the glory of God" (Romans 3:23). And our sins have separated us from God (Isaiah 59:1). All mankind has been separated from God and has gone under the bondage and rulership of Satan.

Satan Is the Ruler and Leader of All Who Have Not Been Delivered from His Bondage

Now the sovereign God, Jehovah, has no choice except to do something to deliver mankind from his bondage to Satan. *Sin* has become such a great influence on mankind to be totally gone away from God and keep them under his bondage. Human mind has become the battlefield between good and evil. Man has acquired this capacity of knowing good and evil after he ate the fruit of tree in the Garden of Eden, which God had forbidden to eat (Genesis 3:1–15). Now man is in the situation to choose between good and evil. Morality demands man being good and righteous because that is the nature of God. Being evil and unrighteous does not demand any morality or moral behavior. God is showing the goodness of the eternal life with the vision of heaven and the joy with which he is going to spend his eternity. Satan is showing all the pleasures coming from the temporal world through the lust of the flesh and the lust of the eyes. The pleasures the world offers overrules the morality, discipline, and the good righteous character of mankind. This battle is going on in the mind of men all the time everywhere in the whole world.

Satan has the complete control of our mind and saturates it with all uncleanness to go after all the pleasures of the world in the form of entertainment. Human mind has been almost shut down to the understanding of good and evil. Human mind is under the control of the devil totally, and that is what the Bible describes as follows. Read Ephesians 4:17–19: "Ye hence forth walk not in the vanity of your mind having the understanding darkened [by the devil] being alienated from the life of God through the ignorance in you because of the blindness of your heart, due to the work of Satan."

This status of mankind is called being under the bondage of the devil. Whether you know it or not (or like it or not), you are under the bondage of Satan. Everyone in the entire mankind is under the bondage of Satan and is being led and influenced by him. There are no exceptions. Being religious, trying to be good, and trying to be righteous and holy are not going to change your character and attitude as long as your leader is the devil. If a Christian tells me, "I am too busy, and I don't have time to pray or read the Bible," I always use to say, "Yes, brother, you are '*b*ound *u*nder *S*atan's *y*oke.'"

Satan has established his kingdom on the earth from day 1 when Adam fell into sin and lost his dominion over himself and the things and matters of this world. Since he has fallen short of the glory of God—meaning the nature, character, and attributes of God—he by himself can never be able to overcome this bondage. He is like the one who is sinking in deep waters of the sea and battling (swimming) to come of it by himself. How long is he going to do that, or could he? Maybe as long as he has mental and physical strength! He needs a rescuer or a Savior.

Why Mankind Is under Suffering and Curse?

Very often we are quick to blame God for our sufferings and curses! But God is not the cause or reason! The *cause* is the devil, and the *reason* is our bondage under him. Satan is the source of all evil, curse, and suffering. He was neither good nor righteous at any time from the time after he was cursed and thrown out of heaven. He cannot stand mankind being happy or living happy. Why did man start seeking after God? Because he was going through sufferings, hardships, sicknesses, etc., not realizing that he has been blinded already to the light and knowledge of God. The sufferings grew more and more because of their own sin and transgressions. As a matter of fact, man asked for it and got it! He chose to go after evil and become the subject of all curse and suffering. Read Genesis 6:5: "God saw that the wickedness of man was great on the earth and that every imagination of the thoughts (mind) of his heart was only evil continually." This is because mankind has fallen under the rulership of Satan and their eyes are blinded. He is the source of all evil and unrighteousness and hence the sufferings. There is nothing good in him and blessing under his rule.

Against the power of Satan and his authority, man cannot fight himself out to be delivered. It is just not possible. You are already in a status of defeat and under his bondage. Your life is not under the leadership or influence of God any more. You have lost the privilege of being the child of God. Every suffering and trouble is from Satan only. Not from God at all. You may ask me now, "How many people living in the same world are not suffering and seem to be living happily?"

Well, it needs complete explanation. God was good and made everything good for man. No suffering, no curse, and not even death. But the devil brought everything in. As long as anyone is under his rule and goes along the way he is showing you, everything appears to be good before your eyes. But all are just illusions and delusions. Nothing is factual. We are being carried away by the outward appearance of everything in front of us looking good. When everything happens the way we like and want, we feel happy. When something goes wrong or happens against our wish, then we start to blame God, blame others, blame the situation, and finally blame ourselves! We never blame the devil (Satan), who is the root cause of these happenings. When you start seeking God in the midst of your sufferings, you oftentimes feel God is away from you and not responding to your call. The truth is not that the truth is our eyes are blinded to the understanding of the provisions of God for us and for the entire mankind to overcome the sufferings and curse brought in by the devil. Even death came because of the devil, and he has power over death until Jesus came and died on the cross, buried, and was raised from the dead, overcoming the power of Satan over the death also.

So never blame God for your sufferings. Learn more in the next chapters.

CHAPTER 2

The Actual Source of Suffering!

Satan is the source of all evil, curse, and suffering. God *is not*. He was neither good nor righteous at any time from the time he fell. He cannot stand mankind being happy or living happy. Why did man start seeking after God? Because he was going through sufferings, hardships, sicknesses, etc., not realizing that they have been brought into his life by Satan and have been totally blinded already to the light and knowledge of God. The sufferings grew more and more because of their own sin and transgressions. As a matter of fact, man asked for it and got it! He chose to go after evil and became the subject of all curse and suffering. Read Genesis 6:5: "God saw that the wickedness of man was great on the earth and that every imagination of the thoughts (mind) of his heart was only evil continually." This is because mankind has fallen into the rulership of Satan and still under it. He is the source of all evil and unrighteousness and hence the sufferings. There is nothing good in Satan and no good blessing under his rule. There is no point in debating or arguing about his existence as the atheists are doing about God. The fact remains that we are living in the world full of sufferings.

The fact we have to find out is whether Satan is ruling the world or God is. There is a universal opinion and belief in all the religions that God is ruling the world and Satan is trying to fight against God and cause evil to happen among mankind. But the fact is the opposite. It is God who is trying to free mankind from the bondage of Satan. It may look strange to you right now. Let me explain.

You know the narration of the incident that took place in the Garden of Eden between God, Adam, Eve, and Satan as recorded in Genesis chapter 3. After the first man and woman were deceived by Satan, God had to intervene and declare a proclamation. God first gave the dominion over all the living things on the earth to the man (Genesis 1:28), not on all the earth and nature. After his fall, God made him an alien to the earth. He has no more dominion or authority over anything on the earth. If he has to live and survive, he has to toil and work hard. God is not going to provide everything for him freely. God has also cursed the earth, and the earth is cursed even until today (Genesis 3:9–19). As long as they were in the Garden of Eden, they don't have to work and till the land but happily eat what God has provided for them there. God provide for all the living things, including animals, like the birds of the air and the fish of the sea, for them to eat and live. Firstly, His provisions were removed, meaning he has to toil and work to make his living. Secondly, His protection has been removed, and he is now directly exposed to Satan's attack in every way. God stopped visiting them in the cool of every day as He was doing before (Genesis 3:8). The direct relationship between man and God is severed. Thirdly, his power and authority was removed. Man lost his power and authority over everything, including the power to resist the evil. It became easy for Satan to corrupt the mind of man and bring him under his bondage. He was only waiting for such an opportunity to seize mankind under his control, and he succeeded. Hence from that day, Satan became the ruler of the world, meaning mankind and world systems, through him.

On the other hand, the rest of the living things (besides mankind) and the entire nature are still under the rulership of God Himself. This explains why and how God is providing everything for every other creature for them to survive in this earth. There were incidences and accounts that, whenever there were natural disasters and droughts etc., other living things including the fish of the sea, the fowls of the air, and everything that moves on the earth died without food but never became extinct by any other means except being destroyed by mankind. Rarely famines or pestilences, even tsunamis, have destroyed much of them. Men die, but the animals and other living creatures escape and survive such unforeseen circumstances and natural disasters. Man is not providing for them or protecting them, but God does. The wise men, those are very closely associated with those living creature, including the psalmist King David, say that they look to their creator for everything and praises Him for all His provisions for them to live. What a wonder! God is still reining but not over mankind because mankind has rejected God and His rulership and embraced Satan's rulership.

Two Reasons to Understand Why God Has No Rule over Mankind!

Because He has given them freewill. In the first instance when Adam choose to disobey God's command, He did not stop him; neither did He immediately reverse everything. The choice was his, and he has to face the consequences. Well, we may argue that man did not know it at that time and the real consequences of it. But he was warned about it. God commanded them not to eat on the fruits of the tree of knowledge of good and evil but can enjoy everything else. Man ignored the warning and chose to disobey the command of God. He lost his dominion over everything and became a slave to Satan. He asked for it and got it! Satan, who was looking for such an opportunity, took advantage of the situation.

This brought in a wall of separation between God and man (Isaiah 59:1). If we carefully read the story of Job, a number of things will come to light. On an appointed time, all the sons of God present themselves before God, and Satan also was among them.

God asked Satan, "Where have you been?"

He replied, "I was wandering to and fro on the earth."

"Did you put your eyes upon my son Job?"

"Yes, Lord, but he is hailing and worshiping you because You have put a hedge around him and protecting him. Now remove that wall of protection from him, you see how he will curse You!"

So it becomes very clear that unless God keeps a wall of protection around you, you are vulnerable for any kind of attack of Satan. This applies to the entire mankind. Who will be protected? Only those who seek His protection. King David knew it very well, and that is why in many of his psalms, he was thanking God for Him being his fortress and shield and refuge (Psalms 46:1).

When Satan asked for permission to allow him to take away every good thing from Job and destroy even his health, he just demanded the protection to be removed. He did not pray to God to take away everything from him and destroy his health. Because he knew he could do it himself and he has the power to do that. God also is aware of it, and He did not or could not stop Satan from doing so because now mankind is under his rulership. Mankind is a slave to Satan. Immediately don't turn around and blame God for this situation! I am going to give the provisions which God has made for it!

He cannot compromise with sin unless duly reconciled. Your sins have separated you from me forever (Isaiah 59:1). All have sinned and come short of the glory of God (Romans 3:23). There is none righteous, not one (Romans 3:10–12). There is none that understands; there is none that seeks after God. They are all gone out of the way (of God); there is none that does good—no, not one! These statements make it very clear that everyone is under the rule of Satan and not God. Jesus Himself said, "You are all sons of your father, who is the devil, and under his rule."

The common question asked is that why not God ignore the acts of men and compromise with them because all of mankind is His own creation? Good question but irrelevant. In the first place, God is holy and fully righteous, and He cannot compromise with any unholy, unrighteous things—the origin of which is sin and Satan. Satan himself originally was not unholy when he was created. Because of his rebellion against God, he was judged and cursed to be evil, whose judgment is already pronounced. He is now total embodiment of evil. Is there any way for him to be reconciled back with God again? *No way.* So from God's point of view, any sin resulting from any act of disobedience will not be tolerated by the holy God. Either it has to be punished or duly reconciled at His standards. Because He could not make any kind of compromise with sin, He had no choice except to give up His rulership of mankind over to Satan. God is holy by His highest standard of righteousness (Isaiah 5:16). Satan can never reach that standard to be reconciled back to God. He is eternally separated. But mankind is not so. God has made a provision by which they can be reconciled back to God. But again, it is purely the choice of men. God will never force anything on anyone nor compel anyone to do what God wants unless they are predestinated to do it, and it is His will to use Him for fulfilling that purpose.

Even in the common course of this world, every crime is subjected to punishment. Supposing every criminal is forgiven and released, on any grounds even on humanitarian grounds, is it justified? Then the whole world will become full of criminals. That is how God found the world to be before He brought the flood and destroyed the whole world, save Noah and his family (Genesis 6:5). God saw the wickedness of man was great in the earth and that *every imagination of the thought of his heart was only evil continually*. So He destroyed all mankind along with all living things and saved only Noah and his family and all the living creatures He wanted to continue to propagate on the face of this earth. God established His holiness and righteousness one more time on the earth.

How did this happen? Satan started attacking the mind of human beings. As we observed earlier, human mind is the seat for Satan's attack and is very vulnerable. He was able to infuse murderous thought into Cain's mind, and he killed his own brother Abel. These kinds of activities continued on and on to an extent that the imagination of the human heart became evil continually. God cannot compromise on that no matter what! So it has become possible for Satan to enslave mankind completely.

Among the early generations, Enoch became an exception. He established a very good fellowship and relationship and lived for three hundred years walking with God (Genesis 4:7–18). Death could not have power over him, and he was transformed into a heavenly being without seeing death. The first person who did not see death was Enoch, and he was able to overcome every temptation of Satan to fall into sin and obtained the greatest testimony that he was one of the two who never tasted death. Because he never tasted death, he is not going to face judgment either. There were many others chosen by God. Noah, Abraham, Isaac, Jacob, Moses, Samuel, David, Isaiah, Jeremiah, Ezekiel, and many other prophets were able to beat the wiles of the devil and overcome him with the help and power of the Holy Spirit. Other than these selected, specific men of God the rest of the world was and is still being ruled by Satan.

Satan's Kingdom on Earth

Babylon became the capital of Satan's kingdom. In the meantime, we also have to understand how Satan established his kingdom on the earth. Let us read Genesis chapter 11. When all men were together in one place, Satan started to work in their minds. He infused the same thought which he had in his mind that lead him to his fall. They (all men) said to one another, "Let us make brick and burn them thoroughly." They started to make bricks for stones and slime for mortar. "Let us build a tower to reach up to heaven, and let us make a name to be equal to God in the highest." Satan was able to maneuver the humans to think proudly by putting the thought into their mind to reach the level of God himself. Although Satan knows that it will not be possible and God will execute judgment immediately, he still tried to achieve his original ambition through mankind. The story goes on and finally to a place called Babel meaning "confusion." God had to intervene and scattered them from that place by confusing their language to different parts of the world.

The city of Babel was later called Babylon (after meaning "the gate of god," with small *g*). This city was first built by Nimrod (Genesis 10:10), one of the great kings recorded in the human history. He was the first king exhibiting satanic characters. Satan had his first king in Babylon which became eventually the capital of his kingdom.

- Babylon had an exclusive glory among the kingdoms at that time (Isaiah 13:19).

- Babylon is the city of beauty of the Chaldeans' excellency (called Chaldees before).
- Babylon was regarded as the golden city (Isaiah 14:4).
- Babylon was called the Lady of the Kingdoms (Isaiah 47:5, 7).

Such was the city of Babylon and the capital of the kingdom of Satan. It was regarded as the capital of all merchandise and the trade center of the world at that time. In due course, it became the sin capital, meaning the headquarters of all major sins like idolatry, adultery, and pride.

Reasons to Prove Babylon Was the Sin Capital of Satan

1. The city was the symbol of *pride* (Isaiah 13:19, 14:4; Jeremiah 50:29–34; Revelation 18:7–8). The city was constructed by Nimrod with a main attitude to make it as the greatest city in the world. He brought in all merchandise and made that city as a great commercial (trade) center. All the valuable merchandise from gold to fine flour was brought in for trading in to this city. As a matter of fact, it was the Babylonian currency which was in use for all kinds of trade activities. Later, the same was shifted to New York, USA, the details of which I will provide in the later chapters.
2. Idol worship (Jeremiah 50:1–2, 51:47; Revelation 9:20–21, 13:14, 14:9–11, 16:2). Idol worship was first introduced to mankind at Babylon. First, they started to build idols for deities. During the reign of King Nebuchadnezzar, he became so proud that he built his own image as a statue and commanded the people to worship his own image (Daniel 3–6). That became the reason for his fall and later the fall of Babylon itself. The Statue of Liberty, which is now the landmark and a monument of the great city of New York, USA, is from Babylon. When the USA was founded, it never had any statue to symbolize their foundation. It was founded on the Judaic-Christian values. They never had

idol worship. This became the second significant icon in American culture derived from Libertas, the goddess of freedom widely worshiped in ancient Rome, especially among emancipated slaves from ancient Babylon. I will give more details in the later chapters.

3. Pleasures, sins, and luxuries (Isaiah 47:8–11, Revelation 18:3–19). As a trade city, it was exposed to the arrival of people from all nations of the world. And they happen to stay in that city long enough to complete the trade for which they came for. During such times, it was customary then and now to entertain them with all kinds of entertainments, the most of which was prostitution. It became women's liberty and the symbol of liberty statue was created as the goddess of freedom to practice prostitution without any legal bindings. Following this sin was practiced like drinking of water in Babylon. Luxuries flowed in because of trades. See how Satan worked out his way to make that his capital on earth.

4. Fornication (Revelation 14:8, 18:3–9). A great voice declared from the heavens, "Babylon the Great is fallen, and because it became the habitation of the devils, and held every foul spirit, and a cage of every unclean and hateful bird. For all nations have drunk the wine of the wrath of her fornication, and the kings of the earth have committed fornication with her, and the merchants of the earth are waxed rich through the abundance of her delicacies."

5. Spiritism and sorceries (Isaiah 47:12–13, Revelation 18:2). When the judgment was proclaimed against Babylon by the Prophet Isaiah, a challenge was called upon like this. "Stand now with your enchantments and with the multitude of your sorceries, wherein you labored from your youth, if so be you shall be able to profit, if so be you may be able to prevail. You are wearied in the multitude of your counsels. Let now the astrologer, the star gazers, the monthly prognosticators, stand up and save yourself from these things which are going to come upon you!"

6. Oppression of Israel. (Isaiah 13:1, 14:2–22; Jeremiah 51:24–25; Revelation 18:24). When God executes justice against Babylon because they oppressed Israel in many ways and at many times. God said through the Prophet Jeremiah to Babylon as under, "I will render to Babylon and to all the inhabitants of Chaldea all their evil that they have done in Zion [to Israel] in your sight." God says "I am against you. I will stretch out My hand upon you and roll you down the rocks and will make you a burnt mountain." The only person against Israel is Satan, and he motivated Babylonians and Chaldeans to oppress Israel, and this tells us that Satan was operating from Babylon, his capital city.
7. Martyrdom of saints (Revelation 18:6, 24). "She (Babylon) has killed many saints and prophets, and their blood is seen in her hands and the blood of the saints all over the earth killed by the wrath of Satan against the people of God."

Thus Babylon became the capital *sin city* of Satanic kingdom. Babylon was the capital for many great kings who rose on the face of the earth, including Nebuchadnezzar. They were more knowledgeable than the rest of the world and were able to rule the greater part of the world at that time. For example, the Hanging Garden built by Nebuchadnezzar by the side of his palace was considered one of the great wonders of the world. From the scientific point of view, such a garden could be successfully created and maintained, and it shows to the world how knowledgeable they were. According to one archeological scientist, it was observed that the garden was an indoor garden and should have been fully air-conditioned.

On the other hand, they denied the true God and started worshiping strange gods and instituted idols for worship. They rejected the God of Abraham, Isaac, and Jacob. They created their own gods and idols and started worshipping them. In Babylonian religion, the ritual care and worship of the statues of deities was considered sacred; the gods reside simultaneously in their statue in temples and in the natural forces they embodied. Thus, the idol worship became a universal ritual practice. I am not going to list the number of deities the worshiped, both male and female, as it is innumerable and of no great importance.

Babylon: The Capital City of Satan

We have been considering how Satan seized the rulership of the world and world systems. He started dominating in the affairs of the world systems because mankind has been totally under his bondage and rule. It became easy for him to establish his kingdom. Men rejected God and good and chose to follow Satan and evil. God had given freewill to men. He can choose anything to follow. Why didn't God stop it or control it? He will not, and He cannot. This may be difficult to understand, accept, and digest, but that is very much true. God was visible and was having fellowship with man in the Garden of Eden, but we lost it because of the sin of Adam and Eve, and He became invisible. Now the greatest blame on God is that He is invisible. And why is He hiding? For someone who does not believe in God, this will look absurd because he doesn't want to understand why it is so. See this is the understanding of an atheist:

> Religion has actually convinced people that there is an invisible man [God] living in the sky who watches everything you do, every minute of every day. And the invisible man [God] has a special list of ten things [Ten Commandments] he wants you to do. And if you don't obey any of these ten things, he has a special place [hell] full of fire and smoke and burning and torture and anguish, where he will send you to live and suffer and burn and choke and scream and cry for ever and ever till the end of time … But he loves you. (George Carlin)

First of all, he is not a theologian or a professor or a yogi or a religious person, and he does not have any authority to comment on something about which he does not have any basic understanding.

He is a comedian or a clown on the stage that makes people laugh in the audience. The comedian is giving an opinion of God and a learned biologist and a professor in one of the renowned universities in England reproduces the comedian's remarks in his book (I don't want to mention his name here). He calls himself a great atheist, quoting in his book this comedian's version of God. What a joke! This is how man understands about God. If he is giving an opinion about a living God like this, how about the millions of people who are worshiping idols and unknown and unheard of deities? And what is going to be his version of them and their deities?

God is actually *not* invisible. He is invisible to our naked eyes. Our naked eyes cannot see and visualize everything. Our eyes have very limited capacity of vision. If you stand near an airport and watch a fight taking off, you see them slowly disappearing from your sight into the clouds, but does it mean that the airplane is not there? It is still flying toward its destination, but you could not see it. You may immediately say, "Well, we don't see it, but we *know* that the airplane is still flying." In the same way, God is there. We are not able to see Him by our naked eyes, but it does not mean He is not there or He does not exist. He does exist, and we can and have to know it.

Man could not see God, and that gave Satan the opportunity to instigate man to create the idols to replace the living God. Wise men did not accept this idea of creating idols in the place of God, and they started searching for God (knowing very well that He is invisible) and how to know and understand Him, and that is why religions came. Then again, they fell short of convincing the people about the existence of God without showing them in some kind of physical form. This ideology has opened easy room for Satan to occupy the human mind and convince him to believe that there is no God and he need not fear to fulfill any moral obligations. Satan knows very well that God demands highest morality because He is holy and righteous. But man wants to be free to do anything he wants, whether good or bad, whether it hurts his neighbor or even God. This is the ideology of Satan. Just follow and do whatever looks good (lust of the eyes), whatever tastes good (lust of the flesh), and whatever makes you to feel great (pride of life). All these three are from Satan, the god of this world, and not from the Father in heaven, who is the *true* God (1 John 2:16). Satan knows that this will please mankind after all. So he started providing everything to satisfy these emotions in his mind. And he got them under his slavery. The god of this world (Satan) has blinded their eyes. Mankind, not realizing the bad and adverse consequences of this, has fallen into this trap. What a loss to mankind and gain to the adversary Satan.

To fulfill his ambitions and desires, he has to establish his kingdom. He should have a capital. He chose Babylon to be his capital. He brought in the world trade to be centered in Babylon. All the valuables of the world (the Bible lists thirty valuable things) were brought into Babylon for trading. The whole world is revolving around economy. Economy is based on trade, so he could control the entire world from Babylon.

The next move is to entertain the traders and merchants coming from all over the world. Then he opened up entertainment to the flesh by way of prostitution. The Bible vividly describes the way Babylon became the headquarters of the world for the sin of the flesh. I will describe this more in the later chapters.

Then the sin of pride of life. The kings of Babylon were exalting themselves more and more than every other king of the world and ultimately exalting over God Himself. For example, in the book of Daniel, we read that the King Nebuchadnezzar put up a golden image of himself, tall and great, and decreed that everyone should bow before that image, or else they will be thrown into the fiery furnace alive (Daniel 3). And we all know the challenge made by the three Hebrew young men who were the children of the Most High God and how they succeeded in that trial. What does it infer to us? Satan is ruling the world and world systems. God's people are always on the defense. Ultimately, by the great and mighty hand of the Lord, the children of God are able to defeat Satan and his army and wiles every time. Satan does not stop there, and he starts something else from some other angle. He never stops just in one occasion when we overcome and defeat him. He comes back again and again.

CHAPTER 3

The Strategies of Satan

The Bible (Paul) calls it as the *wiles* of the devil (Satan) (Ephesians 6:11). Satan had his own strategy to bring down mankind to the roots of evil and turn them against God. He knows pretty well that God is holy and righteous and will never compromise sin, evil, and unrighteousness. As a matter of fact, he knows the character of God more than you and me because he was a cherubim and one of the archangels whom God had created. He spent enough time in heaven to know and understand God fully well. When he was given the rulership of the then earth, the earth before Adam and Eve were created (Genesis 1:1–2), his attitude changed. There are enough evidences to prove that he was ruling the then earth and all the living creatures in it. The cherubim and other angels were not created in the image of God or His only begotten Son, Jesus Christ. Their description does not match either the image God or the image of man. God created man in His own image, and later He created woman to be a helpmate for him. That may be the reason why God hates the images of woman deities or goddess. I don't mean that God does not respect women, but when the image of God was likened unto a woman in many religions, it became an abomination to Him. For Satan, also it has become easy to deceive women as by nature they are weaker vessels (1 Peter 3:7). This is also one of the reasons that the Bible likens Babylon to a woman and so on.

Eve Was Deceived First

Consider what Paul writes to Timothy (1 Timothy 2:13–14). Adam was first formed, then Eve. Adam was not deceived, but the woman being deceived was in the transgression. Satan was well aware that he could deceive the woman more easily than man. When Peter writes that women are weaker vessels, he does not mean to grade them weaker, but in the creation itself, she was created to be a helpmate for the man because she was formed from the bone taken out of man. She was meant to be equal to man in every respect in being a good and perfect companion, not with a motive of claiming equality in everything, including exercising authority over man or trying to obtain headship over man. (I will explain this more in the coming chapters.) In view of this, Satan did not want to approach woman, not when she was with Adam, but met her privately when she was alone. He is a deceiver from the beginning, and he will only look for opportunity and perfect situation. He just planted a seed of doubt even when God commanded her to stay away from eating the fruit of the tree of knowledge of good and evil. He achieved most of his plans by deceiving and at perfect situations. She did not consult her husband (Adam) before eating the fruit from that tree and gave it to Adam after eating it herself. Adam also ate it, not doubting about it, and their eyes were opened. This was his first attempt to defeat mankind, and he succeeded.

Sarah Was Deceived to Offer Hagar to Abraham

I was always very reluctant to say this to the Christian believers' community. She was regarded and respected as the mother of all believers. I respect that belief without any dot of doubt. God did promise Abraham and Sarah that their seed only will be the recipient of God's promises. Abraham believed it and was waiting patiently. His faith was not wavering. But Sarah's faith wavered, and Satan made use of the situation to deceive Sarah for the following reasons:

When God intervened Satan in the Garden of Eden, He cursed and challenged him and said as follows in Genesis 3:15: "I [God] will put enmity between you and the woman and between your seed and her seed. He will bruise your head, and you will bruise his heel." There was enmity created between the woman and Satan. Satan knew very well that it is the line of Abraham God has predestined the birth of Jesus, who is going to bruise his own head. He could not do anything else except to counter him through the seed of Abraham himself. He started scratching his head and crushing his brain to find a way to counter Jesus. He also is aware that he cannot stop Jesus from coming into this to destroy his activities.

Read 1 Timothy 3:15. So what is the other alternative? Somehow, he wanted to destroy the image of Jesus and fight against His purpose for which He is going to into the world. Satan decided to deceive Sarah, the woman and the weaker vessel, and entered into her mind.

The situation gave him the opportunity to execute it easily. He told Sarah, "Hi! You are getting old. You are not going to bear a child for Abraham. Maybe Abraham also is growing older and older as the years run by. Maybe it will be God's plan to get a child through Hagar for yourself. After all, she is your handmaid and she will agree to this to please you and her master Abraham. Why don't you try this method? Maybe it is God's will too!"

Alas, Sarah is trapped! She thought, "Maybe it is a very smart idea! Why don't I try it out?" Satan always never reveals to anyone the consequences of any of his deceptive ideas or suggestions. At this point, where did her faith go? When I read the account of Sarah's faith in Hebrews 11:11, I was able to understand it better. Through faith, before and after this verse, Paul wrote always that *by faith* everyone obeyed God. Only in the case of Sarah, Paul writes that she first received strength to conceive seed and delivered a child when she was past age, and later *judged God to be faithful* who had promised. This faith she acquired after Abraham was able to give a child to Hagar. After Hagar had the child by Abraham, again, the second time the angels of God visited him and confirmed to him that Sarah is going to have a son according to the time of life. Sarah did not believe it either but laughed over it! Then again God had to confirm it to her by another promise: "Is there anything too hard for the

Lord?" (Genesis 18:9–15). Maybe she started believing in the power of God's promise now and was able to bear Isaac.

Satan Achieved What He Wanted through Ishmael, Hagar's Son

For many of us, it may look surprising to know the great thing which Satan has achieved through Ishmael. The rivalry began between Israel (Sarah's descendent) and Ishmael (Hagar's descendent) right from there and is continuing till today, and it will continue until Jesus comes back. This is what Satan wanted and got it done by deceiving Sarah! Abraham was not willing to cooperate with this; it was Sarah who persuaded him to agree to this. Later when Hagar raised her voice against Sarah, she realized her mistake, but it is too late. She forced Abraham to get rid of Hagar and son Ishmael. This hurt Abraham's feelings. After all, Ishmael also is his own blood and son, and he prayed to God, saying, "God, let Ishmael also live before you!" God heard Abraham's petition and also remembered the promise He gave to Hagar in the wilderness. He was forced to bless Ishmael with all material blessings and his generations to multiply greatly in the world, but held and reserved all spiritual promises and material blessings to the generations through Isaac to Israel. What did Satan achieve?

1. He got Ishmael through Abraham himself. Now he is Abraham's seed.
2. He was able to get God to bless Ishmael, too, in accordance to His promise to Abraham.
3. He was able usher in a rival generation for Israel. Ishmael brought forth twelve great princes and kings through them on the earth. Because he was Abraham's seed, God had to or forced to bless him on two grounds. Firstly, God had promised Abraham that through him, many nations will rise, and they will be blessed materially in this world. But the spiritual blessing (salvation and eternal life) was not promised to that generation, and they have to find it like

any other gentiles in this world. Secondly, God heard the prayer for Ishmael by Abraham and answered it (Genesis 17:18). Abraham pleaded before God that Ishmael also should live before you in this world. And God granted his request. But the enmity and rivalry was not removed between them. Throughout the history, we find the rivalry is continuing between these two generations, and it will not end until Jesus comes back.

4. He was able to bring out the great rival for Jesus Christ in the generation of Kedar, the second son of Ishmael (Genesis 25:13), Mohammad Nabi, but that was too late because Jesus has already completed the purpose for which He came. Satan's plan was defeated in that attempt.

5. Through Islamic religion, he was able come against Judaic-Christian communities throughout the world. Now the ultimate goal is to take over the entire world system and deceive the entire world. We all know how Christians are being persecuted and are going through untold sufferings throughout the world for the name of Jesus Christ by the descendants of Ishmael.

6. Satan knew that he will be able to keep the generations through Ishmael under his control throughout and accomplish everything he wants through them. We are able to see how Satan is able to radicalize all the followers of Islam with a false hope they all will be rewarded to satisfy the lusts of their flesh but never will give the real and proper understanding of salvation and eternal life of their souls. We can openly see this happening all over the world.

7. Finally, he is going to usher in the antichrist from the Ishmael's Islamic generation. The antichrist will be the final attempt by the devil to stand against Jesus Christ and against the kingdom of God.

Not knowing Satan's plan and strategy, Sarah fell in his trap. Many theologians and Bible scholars may think and explain it otherwise. We have to take into consideration that God did not stop

Satan to deceive Eve; there is no surprise that God did not stop Satan to deceive Sarah too. She became the mother of all the faithful after she realized that she had committed the greatest blunder (something against God's will and plan) by offering Hagar to Abraham and later even forced Abraham to disown her. But it was too late. After her realization, God did accept her to be the mother of all the faithful because of His original plan to bring Jesus the promised seed through Sarah by Abraham. Here again we have another proof that Satan is the ruler of mankind and through him the entire world.

Two Great Weapons Satan Used against God: Lawlessness and Idolatry

Lawlessness. Satan is an embodiment of sin and evil. He fell by rebelling against God, and he was cursed and condemned and is being judged accordingly. He is the source of all evil and lawlessness. He deceived Adam and Eve and made them father of all sins and sinners, including you and me. We have to read the first three chapters of Romans very carefully and try to understand the real message Paul is trying to convey. Read Romans 3:11–13. There is none (no one in the whole world as long as they are under the rulership of Satan) that understands or seeks after God. There is no fear of God either. Everyone (irrespective of nationality, caste, color, or creed) has gone away from God, and *no one* is found to be doing good from God's point of view. No one is righteous either. Verse 23 says that all (meaning all humanity or mankind) have sinned and come short of the glory of God (meaning there is no more glory that rests in man when he was first created without sin). From the fall of man until the time law was given through Moses, there was no knowledge of sin at all. Everyone was living in sin, not realizing that they are living in sin. The knowledge of sin came only after the law was given. God had to make men understand that all transgressions are because of lawlessness and sin.

In the days of Noah, God saw that the wickedness (transgressions) of man was great in the whole earth and that every *imagination* of the *thoughts* of his heart was evil continually (Genesis 6:5). As we have been learning that Satan has seized the rulership of the world, it became very easy for him to influence the minds of men to do whatever they liked to fulfill the lust of their flesh. So Satan brought in lawlessness into mankind. It was very easy for him because there is no knowledge of sin at all. When there was no law, transgressions were not considered as sin. There was no fear of God in them in those days. If there was some knowledge of God at that time, there would have been some fear of God. If there was some fear of God, there would have been some righteousness and at least a tendency to do good works and hate evil. Satan had totally taken away any slightest idea about God until God chose to destroy the whole world saving only Noah's family among mankind. They were mocking both Noah and God, but then at that time, when God destroyed the whole mankind, He made a covenant with Noah that He will not destroy the world again by flood like this but would prepare a way through Jesus Christ for redemption and reconciliation.

Satan never stopped working to let go mankind. He started working more vigorously to enslave mankind and bring lawlessness into their day-to-day life. He knows very well that God hates unrighteousness, immorality, and lawlessness. If he wants to take mankind against God, the only and the best way is to take mankind into total lawlessness. Lawlessness will take them toward immorality, ungodliness, and unrighteousness. At the same time, it will take them away from God. In due course, it will bring into their mind a false sense of satisfaction and totally forget God. Satan's strategy is to satisfy the mind of a man in lawlessness so that he will not just forget God but hate God. Lawlessness is an abomination to God. When God found that lawlessness is the root cause of all transgressions, He gave the law through Moses in the form of Ten Commandments.

Even though God proved His own will, plan, and purpose by giving the law, the Israelis did not understand it. Satan has blinded their eyes. He was able to work even in the mind of Miriam, who is his own sister, to mock him by these words. "Has the Lord indeed has spoken only by Moses?" (Numbers 12:2). Then we find in verse 9 the anger of the Lord was kindled against them! This thought (pride of life) originated from Satan, and Aaron and Miriam became victims of this deception. Satan's deceptive tricks did not work with Moses. God, who knows the hearts of all men, knows the thoughts originating in the mind of men, and He will deal with it accordingly. He is a sovereign and righteous and holy God.

See how Satan is slowly and deceptively bringing lawlessness into the present-day society through culture. Under the banner of liberty, he is slowly bringing in lawlessness into the society, states, and nations. Those punishable transgressions few years ago are considered as no more punishable crimes. Lawlessness is taking the central stage in the so-called developed societies and nations. Law and order is quickly disappearing. This is the major end-time strategies of Satan as from the beginning. But at the same time, when it crosses the boundaries which God has kept for them, He brings the end.

Paul, the great Apostle and servant of the Lord Jesus Christ, says like this. He says, "I would not know sin but by the law." For example, I had not known lust is sin, except the law says, "Thou shall not covet" (Romans 7:7). I did not know stealing is sin but by the law which says, "Thou shall not steal." So the law is required for the knowledge of sin. But now Satan is influencing the minds of mankind, that when the law is no more in practice there is nothing which could be called sin, and you are at liberty to do anything you want or feel like doing. His final strategy is to bring in and establish total lawlessness into present society. Under the term *liberty* and human rights, he is removing law and order from the society. Culture is the tool he is using (post-modern culture). Civilization is misquoted to represent the present culture.

Actually, the civilization should take us to a better culture. But he is taking the whole world back into lawlessness under the banner of civilization and becoming modern. For example, improper practice of sex is having no more a limitation or a punishable crime in the present culture. Adultery, prostitution, and abortion are considered *no more* to be transgression or lawlessness or crime and punishable under law. They are slowly getting legalized all over the world. Once it becomes legalized, no human-made system can punish them under any law, but from God's perspective, it is considered as a punishable (transgression or sin) crime, and one has to face the judgment in due time. On the other hand, being pro-life is considered as a victim-less crime punishable under the law of liberty and human rights. Jude puts it rightly: "Behold, the Lord [Jesus Christ] with ten thousands of His Saints, *to execute judgment* and to convince all that are ungodly deeds which they have ungodly commuted, and of all their hard speeches which ungodly sinners have spoken against Him. This includes all those who are walking in their own lusts" (Jude 14–15). Satan is preparing a lawless world society, taking them toward the end of the time of the world systems.

Idolatry. This is the second great weapon Satan was using from the early life of mankind after their fall in to sin and was separated from God. The separation from God and His presence caused a great deal of loneliness to man. He was left on his own. Did God interfere with any of his activities? *No!* He started minding his own business, started tilling the ground for producing food for himself as life has become dependable on one. Other natural and normal activities started to happen, and they started producing children and multiplying on the face of the earth. Was God with them? *No!* Who was on the earth interfering and influencing their life? Satan and his angels! He was operating as an external influence in the lives of mankind. Man's mind does not stop working. He has a mind to think and a heart to feel emotions. He is now an independent personality given the freedom the think on his own and do them and try to execute everything he desires.

There were two sons born to Adam and Eve in the first time. Their names were Cain and Abel. Consider these two men and how Satan intervened and influenced one of them. They did have the thought of God in their minds. Hence, they brought the sacrifices to God. Cain was the tiller of the ground, and he brought the first fruits of the ground as an offering. Abel was the rarer of the sheep, and he brought a firstling of a sheep as a sacrifice to God. So far everything went on well. But God accepted the sacrifice of Abel and *did not accept* the offering of Cain. The Bible never says that God rejected Cain's offering. You may argue and say, "Hey! Look, when something is not accepted, it means it is rejected only!" No! Not from

Gods point of view. God wanted to make Cain understand that, son, you need a sacrificial offering, because now you are a sinner and you need to bring an offering to wipe away your sin. See what God had said! "*If* you do well, will I not accept it? If you do not do well, *sin* will be still lying at your door!" (Genesis 4:3–8). God said to Cain go and bring the right offering like Abel. Because he did not have any knowledge about the right and acceptable offering, God helped him to understand it! But Satan deceived him yet again.

But what happened? Satan came in and occupied the mind of Cain. He said to him, "Look, Cain, you are the firstborn and the eldest! See, God is showing partiality. He has a soft corner for Abel. He loves him and hates you! Don't you see that? Now you have to get rid of him in the first place. Otherwise, you will be in trouble all your life by and through him."

Cain asked Satan, "How could I do that? I don't know how to get rid of him."

"Come on, Cain, you know you were naked but not telling him the truth that he realized he was naked because of his sin. But now you're clothed! How? You have to kill a lamb [animal] and use its skin to cover your nakedness."

"Is that correct?"

"Yeah! Yeah! Then do the same thing to your brother Abel! Kill him!" Satan kindled his emotions and put the corruption into his mind. Cain arose and slew him (Genesis 4:8). Then God saw he committed a sin again. He cursed Cain more. This is exactly what Satan wanted, and he achieved it. Many times, Satan offers apparently good and easy solutions but never will tell you the real consequences of it. This is the kind of deceptions Satan often uses in everyone's life even now. Mankind, not realizing it is the devil who is maneuvering from inside your mind, falls in to his trap and gets into more trouble, particularly the children of God. Beware of Satan's wiles!

When and where did the idolatry come in? Men began to multiply on the face of the earth. After Noah in the generations of Ham, Nimrod was born. He became a mighty man of valor. He built his kingdom in Babel. In the generation of Shem Asshur was born (Genesis 10:1–8, 22), Asshur built the city of Nineveh. Japheth had seven sons. Three of them became great nations. Magog, one of them, built present Russia. Madai built Persia. Javan became the progenitor of Greeks, Italians, and Spaniards. Long before God gave the Ten Commandments, idol worship began to happen. How? God has now become invisible after man fell into sin. There was no more direct relationship with the only true God. Mankind is now wanderers, someone who roves and roams about aimlessly and thinks or speaks irreverently, illogically, and confused. They have almost forgotten God. Their thoughts were to make a name for themselves (Genesis 13). This was the right time and opportunity for Satan to work in the mind of men. At the back of his mind, he did not forget the existence of God because he knows it very well. Now he has to replace God in the minds of the men. He gave them the idea of idols in order to have some object right in front of them to see, adore, and worship in the place of God because God is not visible. But no one has seen God to give a description of Him. He also was aware of the fact that God will hate this idea. But he wanted to do it in order to mock and disgrace God.

It was easy for Satan to introduce idol worship in the mind of man. The psychological nature of man is to look for someone greater than him. This character you can observe in every common man. But there were always exceptions. The man who thought himself is greater than the others became leaders, rulers, and then the kings. Not everyone aspires for such exceptional positions. Once someone becomes a hierarchy individual, he tries to subdue the rest of the people and becomes their head and in due course their king. The rest of the people are willing to be slaves under him and serve him loyally. This natural character helped Satan a lot. The thought and understanding about some superior being over mankind was always there at the back of their mind in every human being. This is because of the environment he is living in. He sees the skies, the sun, and the moon, the stars, all the animals moving around, all the birds flying in the skies, the fishes in the seas, and the plants all over the earth. It caused him to think—after all he did not create any of them but they are all existing! How? There should be some supernatural being that must have done all this. At that time, man could not address that supernatural being as God for lack of knowledge and understanding. Until Jesus came, God was invisible.

This was the right moment for Satan to usher in the idea of idols. He thought it is the right opportunity to play God. He started working in the mind of mankind. Hey! Look! You are looking for some supernatural being that could have created all these things, including you. But he is not visible. So you better start worshiping all supernatural things as God. Look at the sun. It should be surely something supernatural, and it very important for all living things in the world, so why don't you start worshiping the sun? Perhaps this is how the sun worship began! Then the thought bothered him because it also disappears during the night, and we can't see it! Now man thought what to do. Then the devil said to him, "Okay! Okay! Don't you worry! Now think God should be like a man." Man did not have any knowledge about the nature of God until Moses wrote the book of Genesis. They do not know fully well at that time. "All right, create an image of your thinking like an image of a man of any size and decorate the image as you wish and place it in a common place, and call that image as god and make a proclamation saying, 'Here is the supernatural being that has brought everything in to existence,' and everyone should worship this image [which later became idol]."

Bel was the chief domestic god of Babylon. Bel was worshipped as sun god. Then they started worshipping planet Venus as Astarte and planet mercury as Nebo. Under the psychological influence of Satan right from the building of the tower of Babel, the idol worship has begun (Genesis 11). There is no surprise in this. This was the same thing what had happened when Moses went up in to the mountain and was not seen by the people of Israel for forty days. We do not know what happened to Moses, but we need someone to lead us. So they made an image of a calf and said, "This is the god which brought us from Egypt." Now they started worshiping the image of the golden calf. When God is not visible, this is what happens.

We often blame Adam and Eve that they fell into sin even though the situation was perfect and it was the period of innocence. They were innocent, but the situation was not perfectly innocent without the presence of sin. Sin was not present, but a sinner was present in the world who was no other than Satan. We know very clearly that Satan existed even before Adam was created on the earth. Neither Adam nor Eve had the slightest clue that there was a character called Satan full of evil and the source of sin was there. God did not warn them either about Satan. But He wanted to *test* them (God had His own reasons why He did so), not to tempt them. But Satan tempted them. Their innocence was the opening for the devil to cause them to sin. Normally, we blame God for keeping the tree of knowledge of good and evil in the middle of the garden and commanding them not to touch or eat the fruit of that tree. God knew Satan was there. The fact of the matter is that God tested Adam and Eve in the Garden of Eden by the act of obedience. They failed by listening to the voice of the devil and disobeyed the command of God. Their innocence did not protect them. It should have been God Himself who protected them, but He did not either. The reason being Satan has not yet been condemned forever, and that has to be fulfilled only by Jesus Christ much later.

When man fell into sin, he was separated from God forever. Because of this, God became invisible for the human naked eyes. But emotionally and psychologically, he knows there has to be a superior being in existence, and we are not able to see Him. So let us make an image in whatever likeness we imagine to express one or more of His imaginary characters so that he will be visible to us and start adoring and worship Him. Thus, the idolatry came into practice. Satan has smeared the existence of God in the mind of man and replaced it with idols. Satan knew very well that God cannot and would not tolerate this. When man began to think about God as a superior being, they did not glorify Him, neither be thankful to Him, but instead, they became vain in their imaginations, and their foolish heart was darkened. Professing themselves to be wise, they became fools and changed the glory of the incorruptible God into an image made like to corruptible man, to birds, to four-footed beasts and to creeping things (Romans 1:21–22). Satan has engraved in the minds of men that idols are gods. He erased the idea that God is incorruptible and living. Thus, idolatry, which began in Babel, has spread to the ends of the earth. Let God open our eyes.

CHAPTER 4

Satan Has Been Judged with All His Spirits but the Decree Is Not Executed Yet

The Bible clearly indicates that Satan has been judged. The decree against him is pronounced. His judgment is double-fold. The first part of the judgment was pronounced by God when he wanted to extol himself to be on par with God (because he knew he cannot reach a status above God), and he was cast down to the ground (earth) (Isaiah 14:12). "I [God] will cast thee [Satan] to the ground so that everyone can see you and know about you" (Ezekiel 28:17). This is the first portion of his judgment. This has been already executed and fulfilled. But he is not destroyed utterly or totally or completely. From heaven, he was cast down to the earth (ground), and he was let loose on the face of the earth to rule the pre-Adamic earth. With his evil nature and character, he destroyed the then world and world systems (Isaiah 14:16–17). The earth became completely desolate. God destroyed the then earth with everything on it by the first flood, and that was the earth we see in Genesis 1:2, totally covered by water. He, with all his spirits, escaped into the midair (second heaven) above the earth but below the third heaven, where God has His throne. This we find elaborately described by Paul in Ephesians 6:11–12.

Now the following are the levels of occupancy of the different kingdoms in the realm of heavens:

- Third heaven: The occupancy of the sovereign God, His kingdom, filled with heavenly beings, including angels as described in the scriptures vividly. God has His throne there.
- Second heaven: Presently occupied by Satan and his hosts and evil spirits and his kingdom. He has no throne there. First, he had his capital city on the earth, namely the Babylon. Over the period of time, the city of Babylon has been destroyed. But elsewhere, he is trying to establish his headquarters (capital). His final focus was on the United States of America. I will give further explanation later.
- Heaven and earth: The word *heaven* in this case simply means the atmosphere immediately surrounding the earth. This includes the air we breathe, the column of air required for the birds to fly, to filter the rays of the sun which could be harmful to the living things on the face of the earth. The earth, on the other hand, is prepared for the all living things and to be ruled by man whom He created. But everything went topsy-turvy, and now the earth is invaded by satanic hosts and ruling mankind (the world and the world systems). The earth continues to be the same.
- Hell below the earth: Hell was not created when the whole universe was created and brought into existence. The earth was not a fireball like the sun. The earth has different strata in its makeup. The middle (center) portion of the earth is made up of fireball like matter whose temperature could reach as high as six thousand degrees centigrade. This is called the Lake of Fire. When this explodes in certain areas and bust open the earth, we call them volcanoes. The temperature of the volcanoes is estimated to be three thousand degrees Celsius. This central fireball-like matter is covered by rocks, mud, and different kinds of soil to make the earth habitable. The top portion of the earth is covered by water, the reason being the surface of the earth should maintain a certain temperature and also the atmosphere thereupon for every living creature to live and survive.

WHO RULES THE WORLD, GOD OR SATAN?

Now Satan has come in to existence. He also was not created as Satan or an evil force against God. He was an angel when he was created. More so, he was the wonderful and most beautiful of all the creatures including the angels God ever created. We all know the story how such an angel became the devil, the bitterest enemy of God (Isaiah 14 and Ezekiel: 28). It has been fulfilled, but still he is let loose to wander the earth to and fro, not forever but for a short time, until the world is judged. He is going to be judged at the end of the world where to lock him up and bring an end to his activities. The Bible says that the hell was not created at the time when the universe was created, but it was prepared for Satan after he became an evil force against God, and for his hosts and his spirits to be punished forever (Matthew 25:41). Where? Beneath the earth! The hot zone beneath the surface of the earth has been reserved for them when the final judgment would be executed.

The second part of the judgment (with reference to this world) over Satan was pronounced in two stages. The first stage was in the in the Garden of Eden. He being totally evil and sinful, he cannot but harm the human race created in the image of God. Maybe he knows the extent of his punishment for rebelling against God, and he was so vehement in taking on the vengeance on all mankind. He had dominion over the earth until God punished him by bringing the flood on the earth for the first time and covered it totally. He knows that he lost the dominion he had over the earth. He with all his spirits escaped into the second heavens, and he is occupying it right now. The entire earth went underwater when God punished him and removed him from the face of the earth, which we see in Genesis 1:2. The Spirit of God was hovering over the earth to protect it from Satan until Adam was created. When God replenished the earth in the creation process as accounted for in the first chapter of Genesis, Satan could not stand the fact that the dominion and authority has now been given to Adam after he was created. He decided to challenge God by deceiving Adam through Eve and regain the rulership over mankind and thus the world.

When Satan deceived Adam and Eve in the Garden of Eden, God pronounced a decree. The judgment pronounced on the serpent really does not matter much. Whether the serpent walks on its belly and eats the mud, we don't need to care about it. But the decree pronounced on Satan is very important. Serpent was only a tool for the devil to approach Eve to deceive her. But to Satan, God said, "I will put enmity between you and the woman and between your seed and her seed, and he shall bruise your head, and you shall bruise his heel" (Genesis 3:15). Even here, the judgment and the decree were not total and complete. He is still let loose and on the go.

His activities were going on freely until Jesus went to the cross. On the cross, Jesus cried out and said, "It is finished." The first stage of the second portion of the judgment was fulfilled. At this stage, Satan was defeated, but again, neither punished nor destroyed. Satan knows after the death and resurrection of Jesus Christ, his time is getting over, and his end is soon approaching. He tried his best to stop Jesus from going to the cross. He failed very badly. Jesus overcame him and succeeded. That was God's plan, and Jesus fulfilled it without any flaw in it. Now Satan has a counterpart greater than him.

Jesus pronounced the second stage of the judgment over Satan. He said, "The Son of Man [talking about himself] came to destroy the works of the devil [Satan]" (1 John 3:8). "He that commits sin is of the devil, for he sins from the beginning. For this purpose, the Son of Man was manifested [Jesus] to destroy the works of the devil" (1 John 3:8). This will be going on until the end of the world and the final judgment. From the time of the victory won by Jesus over Satan on the cross until the end of the world, the children of God play a major role in resisting, combating, controlling, and defeating the works of the devil in the name of Jesus. These signs shall follow them that believe. Mark 16:17 reads, "In My name they [the children of God] shall cast out devils." We will have constant encounter with the devil throughout our life in this world after we are saved. We can face him, resist him, and overcome him by the authority of Jesus Christ and the power of the Holy Spirit. Jesus also said that the whole world is going to be judged by Him at the end of the world. When the whole world is judged, the ruler of this world (Satan) also would be judged finally. This final judgment is reserved for the whole world and also Satan and his battalion together. Hell is prepared for them for their eternal judgment.

The Prince of This World (Satan) Is Judged

Who is the prince and god of this world? Obviously, Satan (John 16:11). He was the reigning prince until Jesus, the Son of God, came to the world. Satan was defeated by Jesus on the cross of Calvary. He has been already judged for eternal hell and damnation. But he is still at large. Why? It does not mean that he is being given time and opportunity to repent and reconcile with God again, by no means. It is similar to the world's justice system in practice today. After hearing about the allegations charged on the accused and the counter argument represented by the accused, a verdict (called the judgment) is decreed by the judge. The decree could be the highest capital punishment, the death sentence! Now look at the verdict or the decree. Although he has been awarded the capital punishment, the decree is not executed immediately. Normally, a time period of six months to eighteen months is given to the victim, and it will also say that he should provide with everything he needs within the legal time limits, including keeping him in good health until the last day of his execution. Doesn't it look so strange? After all, he is going to die by execution. You inform him of the proposed date of his death and let him live for some period of time? Why? Fortunately or unfortunately, the justice system works that way!

In the same way, the prince of this world is judged. The decree also is pronounced, but the time of the execution of the judgment is reserved for a later day when God decides to bring an end to the world and world systems. The only difference is that he is not bound or jailed but let loose to have his way until that day. He is still acting as a prince of this world but has an opponent who are strong enough to *resist* and *defeat* him with the *one* (Jesus) who has already defeated him on the cross with the power of the Holy Spirit.

Babylon the Great

Through the previous chapters, we learnt that Babylon was the capital city of Satan on the earth and it was also rightly called the *sin city*. The sins and the abominations against God was originated from here and spread all over the world. The whole world also had the opportunity of gathering in Babylon from time to time for trade and merchandising, and it was easy for Satan to spread the wings of his rulership around the world. Hence, Babylon was recognized as the great city of the world. Great kings ruled from there, including the generations of the great king called Nebuchadnezzar, starting from King Nimrod, who built the city of Babel, which was later renamed as Babylon, the sin capital of Satan, the prince of the world. We also have a long history of how the people of God, namely the Jews and Israelites, were captured and brought to Babylon as captives and slaves.

The city of Babylon was known for its greatness in two accounts. Firstly, it was the great capital for trade and merchandising. Secondly, it was known for idolatry and adultery. When we say adultery, it includes all kind of sexual immoralities. Both these sins are abomination to God. Satan was promoting and propagating these sins throughout the world, proving that he is the prince of this world.

We start seeing the prophecies about Babylon and its fall right from Isaiah 13:1. First, God said He will raise Medes and Persians according to Daniel chapter 5. The destruction of Babylon took place during the days of King Belshazzar's regime. King Belshazzar in his dream he saw a handwriting on the wall the following scripts. "MENE! MENE! TEKEL, UPARSIN!" (Daniel 5:25). There was no one but Daniel who could interpret that dream. This is the interpretation of the thing: MENE: God has numbered your kingdom (of Babylon) and finished. It appeared twice to confirm it as well as to make the king understand that it is going to happen soon. TEKEL: The king was weighed in the balance and found to be wanting. UPARSIN (PERES): Your kingdom is going to be divided and given to Medes and Persians.

Even before Isaiah prophesied about the destruction of Babylon, Sennacherib, king of Assyria, captured Babylon and wanted to destroy it, but he didn't destroy it completely. There were some ruins. Sennacherib's son became king in his father's place and decided to rebuild it over the ruins, and he did it. When God has decided in His mind to destroy the kingdom of Babylon, it was the rebuilt kingdom of Babylon, and the Babylonians started to become powerful again. This was the kingdom prophesied by Isaiah that would be destroyed by Medes and Persians. This was the time Babylonian empire was totally destroyed and scattered all over the earth as described in Daniel 5.

Why then in the book of Revelation Babylon is referred to Mystery Babylon? The simple answer is Babylon is destroyed in 539 BC, but still through the book of Revelation, the name of Babylon is carried on but addressing it as Mystery Babylon. The names of Britain and USA are unheard of at the time of prophecies of Isaiah, Jeremiah, and Daniel, or even at the time of Jesus and John. Only the names were not spelt out; the descriptions are. For example, the prophets must have seen an airplane taking off from the earth (or a spacecraft) and flying so high, and the prophets describe that "even if you fly like an eagle, build your nests among the stars, still I will bring you down." With the background of the Mystery Babylon, it clearly points to the present-day USA. Read further to understand it in the light of prophecies and the book of Revelation.

Which Is the Present-Day Babylon? (The Mystery Babylon)

It might be very surprising to consider the following comparison of Babylon to the present-day United States of America. The greatest of the North American countries is the USA, and it is also recognized as the country in the world. But it is not found or referred in the scriptures (Bible) at all. Many theologians and other Christian spiritual leaders also take it easy any say USA was not in existence in the days of prophecy even until the end of first century, including the days of Jesus Christ, and that is why it did not find any place in their prophecies. It just tells us how ignorant they are regarding the scriptures. When the Bible contains prophecies until the great white throne judgment and the final execution of the judgment over the whole world and over Satan and his battalion in the lake of fire, how come we simply ignore that there are no prophecies concerning the British kingdom and later the formation of USA. If we search the scriptures, we could find a number of references about Britain and USA. After the fall of Babylon and its destruction, the history of Babylon did not cease or end. Neither was Satan silent or inoperative. Every description in the prophecies matched exactly to Britain and USA.

The United States of America is considered to be the present-day Babylon. There are a number of prophecies focusing on the identity of the USA in terms of Mystery Babylon. You may think that there is no relevance or concurrence in the name Babylon and the USA. It may be very true. But in Revelation 17 and 18, John uses only the name of Babylon when judgment has been proclaimed against the last kingdoms on the earth. Virtually, the kingdom of Babylon has fallen well before 650 BC. And after that, the kingdom of Babylon was never built up; the name Babylon was never referred in the history except in the prophetical books in the Bible. Isaiah, Jeremiah, Daniel in the Old Testament and the prophetical book of Revelation has been referring only about Babylon. We have learned from the previous chapters that Babylon was the sin capital and the capital city of Satan on the earth as against Jerusalem, which was and is the capital city of God's kingdom on earth.

The present city of Bagdad in Iraq is the location of the old city of Babylon in the ancient history. We have to follow the history in order to understand this. For the purpose of understanding, we may recon that the ancient Babylon later became the capital of Iraq under the name of Bagdad. But Bagdad never became the city which attracted world trade or the greatest sins of idolatry and adultery leading to open prostitution. No world organizations were established in Bagdad in the present Iraq. The reason being Satan shifted his activities from Babylon to some other city which had better access to the rest of the world. Always remember, Satan is the ruler of the world and world systems. The city of Rome was just then being built with improved architecture and construction methods. It was founded by Romulus, then king of Persian colony, after his name. Rome was growing while Babylon was deteriorating. The Medes and Persians completely destroyed Babylon and started building Rome, which was then a Persian colony. After the Babylonian empire fell, the Roman Empire began. Satan moved his headquarters from Babylon to Rome.

The Roman Empire was strongly established under Augustus Caesar in the year 27 BC. This has very close connection in the birth of Jesus as recorded in the Bible. It was during the time of Tiberius Caesar; Pontius Pilate was the governor of Judaea when the story of the birth of Jesus begins. Now Rome became capital city of Satan for all his operations. The Roman Empire spread to most part of Europe and was very strong for over 1,200 years. In yearly periods of the Roman Empire, Jesus was crucified under the supervision of the Roman tribune and the soldiers. Later in the early 4th century, Constantine became the Roman emperor. Constantine's mother became a very good Christian and slowly converted Constantine to Christianity, and later he made Christianity to be the official religion of the Roman Empire. As a consequence, Catholicism was born, and papacy system was ushered in.

Unfortunately, the Catholicism was not founded on the Christian teachings and values. The emperor was the political head who governed the country, and the pope was the religious head which was almost a parallel authority except the levy of taxes and run the government, taking care of the needs of the people and going for wars, expansion of the empire limits, and promoting cultural and literacy values. Rome was the political capital of the Roman Empire, and Vatican became the religious headquarters of the papacy. On the religious grounds Papacy became an equally great powerful entity extending to the larger part of the world. When different emperors rose and fell, only the empire suffered the loss and the consequences, but the papacy was growing stronger and stronger.

For the purpose of our study, we are going to concentrate on the rise and fall of the Roman Empire. Many emperors arose and extended the Roman Empire to a vast area in Europe into Germany, France, Spanish empire, a major portion of Persia and Greece, and all the leftover of the then Babylonian Empire. Finally, the Romans invaded the Scotland and England and established their colonies there. The colonial system of acquiring and expanding the kingdom began when Romans acquired British Islands and called them as

Scottish and British colonies. It was not named as Roman colonies. They started to have their own governments, cultures, and developing their own national values, except that they were paying tributes to the Roman government. Thus, British Empire came into existence. We will further continue in the next chapter.

CHAPTER 5

The Methodology of Satan's Rule: The Formation of the British Empire

Until 1496 AD, the England and Scotland were two kingdoms severed from the Roman Empire. In 1496 King Henry VII of England got the taste of invading Spain and Portugal. By the time, the Roman Empire had almost deteriorated and shrunken. The British started to gain more political strength. Toward the later part of the sixteenth century, under the reign of Queen Elizabeth I, the British Empire was established in 1583. They brought America and Africa and other thirteen colonies under their control and slavery system to develop America was brought in. Until 1783, British was expanding its empire by colonial system. All these colonies were in North America, Central, and South America. But they lost these thirteen colonies from 1760 to 1770. In 1783, East Asia Company travelled around the globe and made their colonies primarily in India and in many other East Asian countries.

Why British Empire is important for our study? British Empire is not made up of one tribe or race of people. It began with the immigrants from most part of Europe. They had the Babylonian and Roman influence in their culture. They adopted the lion symbol as their national symbol. The surprising thing in this according to historical evidences is that the British people have never seen a lion. Lion was not found in England. How did they acquire the lion as their national symbol? There are a number of explanations given for this. But for our study purpose, it is the direct influence of Babylonian culture, because lion is a Babylonian symbol. Now Satan switched over his operational headquarters to Britain. Surprising? But it is true. Satan is still the ruler of the world and world systems. He is directing all the operations through his people.

The Britain took the lion as their royal symbol. The lion was the symbol of Babylonian. The history reveals that there was no lion in the land of Scottish and British Empires as they were being formed. Their people have never seen a lion and knew nothing about its character. How did they use the lion as their royal symbol? It was the absolute influence of the Babylonian Empire. The prophecy books describe every action of Satan to the activities of Babylon because Babylon was the sin capital of Satan from the beginning. Although the physical Babylonian empire is destroyed by the Medes-Persia invasion, the Babylonian influence is carried on all the way through Roman Empire to British Empire. It is believed that the first pair of lions was brought to England from South Africa after it became a British colony much later.

When the Roman Empire invaded the British Islands, on the religious front, the Roman Catholicism also spread their wings into the British Empire. It was considered as the religion of the British monarchy. During this time, the great reformation took place under Martin Luther against the Roman Catholicism in 1517. At that time, King Henry VIII was the king of England, and he made the Protestantism as the religion of the British United Kingdom in 1534 against Roman Catholicism. Thereafter, under different denominations, the Protestantism, which includes Lutheran Church, Methodist Church, Baptist Church, and Brethrens, got involved in extensive evangelism and missionary work and established Protestant churches all over its empire. The United Kingdom embraced Pentecostalism since 1905 in the early twentieth century and started to grow very fast through evangelism in their membership. Part of the non-Pentecostal mainstream churches embraced Charismatic movement from late 1960s. There is a misunderstanding that Pentecostal churches slowly changed to Charismatic movement. Charismatic movement is just an emotional spiritual movement and not true Pentecostal churches. The true Pentecostal churches continue to stand in their own convictions on the doctrine of Holy Spirit baptism and in the manifestation of gifts of the Spirit as recorded in 1 Corinthians 12.

Since 1760 America started developing and growing rapidly under the British monarchy rule. The king of England, George III, was controlling the American colonies. The American Revolutionary War, also known as American War of Independence, began in 1775 and went on through 1783. On July 4, 1776, the America declared independence in Philadelphia, Pennsylvania. But the fight against the royal British kingdom went on till 1783 when America became a completely independent nation under the name of United States of America. Why it is important? This country was founded on Christian values. Bible was their guiding instruction and law book. The slogan of "In God we trust" appeared in their currencies, the American dollar. For some time, the British pound was recognized as the world currency, as was the Babylonian currency known as Babylonian shekel. But after America became dominant in the growth of economy, military, and world trade, the American dollar became the accepted world currency by every nation in the world.

Although America became independent and was growing strong, the British were still spreading its operations among the rest of their colonies all over the globe. They were concentrating their attention to East Asian countries. Their focus was mainly on India. It was during this period United Kingdom exalted itself and pride took over their minds.

In 1829, when King George IV was king of the United Kingdom, one of his writers in his palace by name Christopher North praised the king with these words. "In Your Majesty's dominions, the sun never sets." The king did not give the glory to God but took it for himself. From then onwards, the British Empire started to decline and fall.

Thus, America became the greatest nation on the earth. Satan started working through the world systems again as before. The world systems are under his control. He exalted America to great heights—in trade, in economy, in military power, in richness. USA made every other country look up to them for growth in every aspect of life of mankind. Finally, it has reached a stage to say, "I sit as a queen [of all nations of the world] and am no widow and shall see no sorrow" (Revelation 18:7). This was the Babylonian pride in those days. USA has reached a stage to say that she (USA) is the queen of the nations. This pride and self-boasting is often called by many as American exceptionalism. This brings out the satanic influence on USA, and how he is going to bring them down to earth will be dealt with in the next chapter.

Present USA in Comparison with the Ancient Babylon

In the book of Revelation, the final judgment is pronounced on Babylon in the last days. But Babylon was destroyed completely, and the name of Babylon itself is totally forgotten by the present world and the world society. Satan is active continuously. After the fall of Babylon, which was the prime sin city of the world, he switched his operations to his new headquarters, Rome. By encouraging the formation of Roman Empire and promoting Catholicism, he was actually working against Jesus Christ. Always we have to remember that God would let Satan to work and do whatever he wants, and at the same time, he fulfills His will, plan, and purpose. Most of the time, Satan is unaware of God's plan and finally gets defeated. Satan has no foreknowledge about the future. In fact, no one knows, including the Lord Jesus Christ and the Holy Spirit as well.

Satan is always cunning and crooked. His greatest weapon is deception. He uses them both physically and spiritually. Unless we are in the Spirit and led by the Spirit, we would never be able to know or understand his wiles and deceptions. They will be very subtle like how he is using the pope and the papacy to deceive the whole world—not just the Christian and Catholics but also the entire world. Everybody thinks and believe that Christianity and the Catholicism are the same. Very few people understand that Christianity is different, and Catholicism is different. Some people even call the Catholics as Catholic Christians. There is nothing like Catholic Christianity or Catholic Christians. When it was formed, it was founded as Roman Catholicism. Jesus Christ was not the core theme of Catholicism. Faith in Christ was not the foundation truth on which Catholicism was formed. "The just shall live by faith" was not their foundation. They adopted pope to be the representative of God, who cannot err and fall, and he has the authority to forgive sins of mankind. This was the greatest deception of all time since the third century until today.

Satan failed in his attempt to kill Jesus when he was a baby. He tempted Jesus so that He might deviate from the purpose for which He came. He attempted many times to stop Jesus from going to the cross, even tried to bring Him down from the cross without suffering the death. He planned many ways to bring disbelief among everybody that did not rise again from the dead. But he could not succeed in anything and failed in every attempt. Finally, He rose again from the dead and prepared the way of salvation for every mankind.

From Babylon to Rome, from Rome to Britain, and from Britain to USA

This is the path which Satan took to control the world and world systems. He was to a major extent successful. In the midst of this turmoil, Christianity has been surviving. Christianity stood the test of time against so many and so great oppositions and oppressions because God was with them. The Holy Spirit who was given to the true Christians on the day of Pentecost has been working with those who have been faithful to God and for the faith in Christ Jesus. When the Roman Empire became the world's most powerful dynasty, Satan was controlling the world and the world systems through them. When the Roman Empire fell and British became the powerful dynasty, Satan worked through them to control the world systems. When the British dynasty fell and USA became the world super power in economy and military might, Satan decided to control the world and world systems through the USA. As I explained to you earlier, God allowed it to happen, but God himself was holding the reign.

When the sin of Babylon reached the heights beyond which He cannot tolerate, He brought destruction over Babylon. It is very much comparable to the destruction of the entire world during the time of Noah and Sodom and Gomorrah during the time of Abraham. God permitted the Roman Empire to become great since 27 BC to bring Jesus in to the world according to prophecies by Moses, David, Isaiah, Micah, and many others. The Roman Empire and the Roman Catholicism started growing stronger and stronger both politically and religiously, moving the world away from God and from Christ. God wanted to bring an end to both these atrocities. The entire thing was maneuvered by the great enemy of God and mankind—Satan. Satan never knew God's plans and propositions.

The Roman Empire had a long history. It was in the fourth century that Roman Catholicism was born. By the end of the fifth century, the Roman Empire was divided into Western Roman Empire, and Eastern Roman Empire. The Western Roman Empire slowly started deteriorating, and British Empire started to dominate the world and world systems. When America was dissociated from the British Empire and became independent, they started growing stronger and stronger and became the world's super power. It was during the same period of time that the Eastern Roman Empire collapsed and Russia emerged as super power of the east since 1721. Satan was not worried about east because it is already under his predominance, but he started to concentrate on the west to destroy and bring it under his control. The east—inclusive of India, China, Russia and South East Asian countries—were not Satan's concern. They are all under his rule already for a long, long time. The west countries—Britain, Canada, USA, and Germany—were involved in evangelism and missionary work for the past three centuries with the gospel of the kingdom of God and practically delivered millions of people from the bondage of Satan, sin and sickness, and curse.

The Revelation of John and the Mystery Babylon, USA

We will have to examine how and why we have to consider prophecies and revelation to understand the Mystery Babylon. The Babylonian Empire fell well before 540 BC. Isaiah prophesied from 792 BC to 722 BC. Jeremiah prophesied from 685 BC to 618 BC.

Daniel prophesied from 610 to 536 BC. All the prophecies of Isaiah, Jeremiah, Daniel are in the timeline of before 536 BC. But when John was given the revelation, the entire judgment is pronounced against Mystery Babylon, and the rationale is very clear that the present-day USA matches with the full description of Mystery Babylon in chapters 17 and 18. Whatever the symbolic visions the prophets had has to be understood in proper perspective. From the Bible point of view, Babylon is the symbol of *sin* and Satan.

For example, Daniel had this vision (Daniel 7:4). The first one was like a lion with eagle wings. The wings were plucked, which tells us that it looked featherless. It is compared to the aircraft or a spacecraft. It was lifted up from the earth, obviously taking off from the earth. It was made to stand upon the feet as a man, and a man's heart was given to it. What else could it mean except to say that Daniel's vision describes aircrafts that are flying and the spacecraft reaching the moon and man setting his feet on it? We all know that it was achieved by man from USA in the middle of twentieth century (1969)

There are a number of exact comparisons of the ancient Babylon to the present-day USA. May the Spirit of God help us to understand them!

USA like Babylon became *astonishment among the nations* (Jeremiah 51:41). USA is just a 230-year-old nation. But how they became the world super power in economy and military is a great astonishment. Their growth in the scientific and technological development is beyond imaginations. In the space research, they are still ahead of every other nation in the world. They put the man on the moon and brought them back safe to the earth. For the people who are living in third world countries, according to the definitions of the UN, USA is a land of milk and honey. They were once described as the *world police*. There was no other single nation to match their might and economic strength.

Babylon versus Mystery Babylon

The ancient city of Babylon (the location is the present-day Bagdad in Iraq) was never surrounded by sea waters, and no trade was taking place via seas. But the present-day USA, known to be the Mystery Babylon, a major portion of which is surrounded by seas and has many deep harbors, company of ships, ship masters, and sailors. A great deal of trade is going on via the sea as described in Revelation 18:17.

If we read carefully from Revelation 18 verse 9–16, we are able to understand how the kings (head of every nation in the world) had dealings with USA and dealt with them so much and made their own nations rich and prosperous (verse 15). The merchants were made rich by her by trading with USA.

On the flip side, they had committed fornication and lived deliciously with her (Revelation 18:9) and satisfied their lust of the flesh because of the cultural changes brought in against God's ordinances and situates. Prostitution was the commonly practiced entertainment for all the merchants coming to trade with Babylon. That is one of the reasons why Babylon was always described and called the Whore of Babylon. Similarly, the present-day Mystery Babylon, which is the USA, is ranking on the top in promoting all practices of sexual immoralities of very kind and now trying to legalize them globally. For example, 60 percent of the world's porn websites are hosted in the USA. Next in the list is the Netherlands at 26 percent. The description is more relevant to say, "All nations have drunk the wine of fornication" (Revelation 18:3). All the rest of the nations of the world share the balance. Isn't it going against God?

The ancient Babylon was constructed by people from all over the world. The USA was also built by people from all over the world, brought in either as slaves or by the people who visited the land, either for trade or for any other purpose.

A major portion of the world's richest people are living in the USA as was in the ancient Babylon. Surprisingly, 48 percent of the billionaires living in the USA are Jews, God's chosen people. God is always keeping up His promises, which He gave to Abraham down to Israel. But if they turn their backs to God, they are punished too, and destruction will come upon the as told by the prophets in the Bible. The destruction pronounced over Babylon will come upon the Mystery Babylon, which is none other than the present USA.

Similarity in the Identity of Babylon and Present USA

The growth of economy, trade, and military power is the mark of the Babylonian Empire. Babylon in the book of Isaiah 47:5 is described as the Lady of Kingdoms. All the kingdoms of the earth were looking up to Babylon as the greatest kingdom on earth at that time. The kings of the Babylonian Empire were so powerful that they were able to bring down all the nations to their feet, including Israel. They have captured the land of Israel many times and took the Israelites as captives to Babylon and looted their temples and took all precious things from their temples, including Solomon's temple. The entire book of Daniel has the full account of Babylonian captivity.

See how the USA has become the greatest nation on the Earth in economy, trade, and military power. Every nation on earth is looking at the USA for trade and selling all their merchandise and for acquiring military capabilities and weapons. In Revelation 18:7, the USA (Mystery Babylon) is described as the Queen of All Nations. USA has exalted itself to great heights. How much she (USA) has glorified herself and lived deliciously for she has said in her heart: "I sit as a queen and am no widow, and shall see no sorrow." The whole prophecy is given against Babylon under the new name Mystery Babylon. The destruction of Babylon was proclaimed when Babylon exalted itself with pride. Now the destruction is proclaimed against USA because America is gone away from God and inviting all the nations (kings) of the earth to commit fornication and live deliciously with her (Revelation 18:9).

Babylon had always been personified to a woman. The goddess of Babylon was called Ishtar. Ishtar is known as the goddess of fertility, love, sex, and war. Her temple was guarded by lions at the gates. In the Babylonian pantheon, she was the divine personification of the planet Venus. Ishtar symbolizes love, including between human and animals, its power and its danger. Under this pantheon goddess, Babylonian custom opened up prostitution, fornication, including illicit relationships between human and animals. Thus, it attracted the kingdoms of the world to visit trade and entertain them by open prostitution. That is why the Bible describes Babylon as the *whore* and caused the world to drink the wine of fornication, which was the sin and abomination against God.

When we consider the cultural and economic growth of the USA, it clearly tells us that it is just the repetition of the cultural and economic growth of ancient Babylon. The outburst of love and sex in the American culture is going back to the old Babylonian culture. The illicit relationship between human and animals are also encouraged. Homosexual relationships are getting popular and are legally getting recognized. Besides economic growth, these cultural developments also attract the nations of the world to come closer to America and practice the same back in their own countries. The description is more relevant to say, "All nations have drunk the wine of fornication" (Revelation 18:3).

The USA has been attracting all nations of the world to offer counsel, support, and cooperation to bring *one world order* under *one world government*. Numerous world organizations have been organized by the USA and have their headquarters in the USA. United Nations, World Health Organization, World Bank, World Court, World Trade Center, and International Monitory Fund are some of them that have their headquarters in the USA. "Thou art wearied by multitude of your counsels, astrologers, star gazers, and monthly prognosticators" (Isaiah 47:13). They bring all world heads of governments and take counsel to bring one world order. After the Second World War, the USA took initiative to bring world peace through the formation of the United Nations under the leadership of Satan, who is their prince and ruler. They don't want to come under the Kingship or Headship of God. God and His statutes are ignored and sidelined. Satanic strategic lawlessness is taking priority. All things which were considered illegal are getting legalized. Satanic another strategy is that "if you want to overcome sin, yield to it." This strategy is loved and accepted overall by mankind. Nobody wants to obey any kind of law, rules, and regulations. Under the banner of liberty, freedom, and human rights, disobedience is considered to be legal, ethical, and their right. To accommodate this lawless attitude, the governments are trying to legalize everything which was once considered to be illegal and crime.

Role of Astrologers, Stargazers, and Prognosticators

I was pondering over the east and the west of the world. To our great surprise, the East—I mean the Eastern countries—are involved in the abovementioned practices for thousands of years. It is totally satanic. Their minds have been totally obsessed with these kinds of practices, and the knowledge of God has been slowly removed from their minds. So Satan is not worried about the Eastern world at all, because they are already under his influence totally. It leads them away to superstitious believes and idolatry. The Western world is not so far involved much in these practices. Their knowledge about God was much different, and they were worshipping the real living God according to their own understanding. But lately, maybe in past last two centuries, these eastern cultural practices are getting more and more popular in all Western culture of life. In the USA, people are getting attracted and involved in astrology, palm reading, soothsaying, and prognostication. The people are curious to know about their future. There are two kinds in this: *foretelling* and *forth telling*. This makes people to feel happy at least for now. Whether all those things are truly going to come to pass or not, that doesn't matter to them.

Do you know that Mr. Ronald Reagan, the former president of the USA, was a great believer in astrology? His wife was always counseling with the astrologers and was advising her husband whenever he was going to make any important decision as president. The Eastern culture is now very strongly getting roots into the Western culture. You will be surprised to know that in Canada, in Toronto alone, the business involving astrology, palm reading, and prognostication is a billion dollar a year business. I am not sure how much is in the USA. This is again the Babylonian practices fully taken over by North America.

CHAPTER 6

What Is Trinity?

The whole Christianity and also the Catholics talk a lot about Trinity, a term which includes the Father, Son, and the Holy Spirit. How many Christians understand the meaning of Trinity? Does anybody know? If so, who is Father, who is the Son, and who is the Holy Spirit? Nobody seems to give a proper or full answer! Many keep saying Trinity is "God is three in one and one in three." This is the *most* irrelevant answer I can think of! The same people will say *they* exist in three different *persons*.

The doctrine of Trinity is the most misunderstood, misrepresented, and improperly explained doctrine. The word Trinity is confusing to so many people, particularly for all those who have no theological background or knowledge. Even for Christians and the believers in Judaism, who strongly believes in monotheism, which means God is *one* according to what has been revealed in the Holy Scriptures, Trinity is a big mystery.

Throughout the Old Testament period, the word Trinity never appears, nor has it any indication. Jehovah is self-existent or the eternal one. Lord is the *only* name by which the true God was known to the people. The plurality exposed and expressed in the creation, particularly in the creation on man, did not give any clue for the understanding of the term Trinity. In the creation of everything else besides man, we find only the singular expression. In every action, we find the term "God said." Only when God wanted to create man the Scriptures uses the term. God said, "Let us make man in our image and in our likeness." Jesus Christ, the Son of God, was still in the form of the Word. When the Word was Spoken, He became the spoken Word with all authority and power. The Word has power in itself. When it was spoken, it has been empowered with *authority*. Now the authority was delegated to the Spirit of God, who is the *chief executive*. He causes everything to come to pass.

In the creation of man, the mode of operation is slightly different. God, with the Word (who later became Jesus) and the Spirit said, "let us make man in our image and in our likeness" in the creative process of man. He formed man out of dust while the Word and Spirit were looking over, and then God breathed into his nostrils. The breath of God had the Spirit to be imparted into man, and he became an immortal soul and represented the individuality and independency of another being like unto themselves. The reason being Godhead comprising of God, Jesus, and the Holy Spirit in reigning and controlling the entire universe in which man was aerated and given authority only over the earth and everything God has put and kept in it. That was the purpose, and that is what He blessed them with. God said to man to be fruitful and multiply and fill the earth and have dominion over every living thing upon the earth (Genesis 1:26–28).

Although the plurality in the Godhead is implied in the beginning and in the creation account, there was no indication to expressly understand Trinity. Even God after the fall of man, when He cursed the man, the woman, the serpent and the earth, He figuratively expressed that God's only begotten Son (then Word) will appear in the due time as Son of Man, born of a woman who will bruise your head and destroy your works. (Genesis 3:15, John 1:14). So it will be more proper to address Jesus as Son of God every time and in every occasion. This does not mean Jesus is recognized as little lower than the Father, the *only* God. When we say "In the name of God," it could probably mean some god of this world and nothing happens. Thing starts to happen only when we use the name of Jesus. To express the superiority in the name of Jesus, we have been taught and told to use the name of Jesus and not generally in the "name of God," which could mean anything, including the pagan gods. Every other creations including Satan and His angels should obey and bow down before the "name of Jesus." Is it that God is going to be jealous over Jesus or the Holy Spirit jealous over Jesus? No way! What a wonderful Trinity if we understand it properly.

All the other gods were known as pagan gods created by mankind for the worship of a supernatural being since it occurred in their mind that there should be a supernatural power existing, and they started to designate that *superpower* as God. In the early years, they believed in a supernatural *power*. They did not know or understand that the power was a personified being. They started designating everything beyond their ability or capacity as God. It was a few people to whom Jehovah revealed Himself and talked with, like Abraham, Moses, and Jacob; only they could realize and understand that the true God is a *person* or a personified being. There was no revelation during the time of the Old Testament that God was existing in three persons, or triune God, or one God existing in *three* different personalities, or three fictionally different entities existed as one person, and so on! Do you think a common or a lay man can understand this? In my opinion, even the theologians do not have one common explanation for this term *trinity*. Everyone has their own explanations, but they don't match with one another, but each of them claim that their explanation is the *only right thing*!

I have done theology myself, done research on this *most disputed topic* myself, and at the end, I could not agree with any of their explanations. To me, it is more and more confusing! If I want to put all the question I had to understand Trinity, all of you will go mad and crazy. I better not do that and confuse you more!

Starting from pope to the lowest clergy in the Catholicism have a very different way of explaining Trinity. In fact, it was the Catholics who coined the word Trinity. They use the most irrelevant method of explaining it. They will simply say "one in three or three in one." They do not know what they are talking about. According to them, Trinity means Father, Son, and the Holy Spirit. They will offer no more explanation to that because they do not know.

Then came the mainline churches (many different denominations like Anglicans, Lutherans, Methodists, Baptists, and Presbyterians) under the banner of Protestant churches who have a number of ways to explain the Trinity. Again, they don't match with each other. The funniest part is each one of them claim that the third person of the Trinity, who is the Holy Spirit, taught them like that or the Holy Spirit revealed it to them in that manner! My humble submission is, if the Holy Spirit according to them is the third person in the Trinity, how could He reveal it differently to the people belonging to different denominations? And finally, the same Holy Spirit says, "Hi, guys, we [Father, Son and Holy Spirit] are all one and the same divine entity! Please understand!" Do you consider all these explanations easy to understand or even more confusing?

Of all the religions in the world, Judaic Christianity has the correct knowledge about God, who is the only sovereign God. This is normally and easily known and understood as monotheism. That is 100 percent correct. Then the next question is, then what is Trinity and how do we explain it? I am not saying there is no Trinity and follow blindly "one God" theory. I believe the existence of Father, Son, and Holy Spirit in the Godhead. The Scripture has clear explanation for Trinity and could be understood very easily.

Just consider the following and think openly!

The normal way of calling Trinity is as follows:

God the Father.

God the Son.

God the Holy Spirit.

They also claim to say all the three are *one*, but functionally, each one is different. If you say they are functionally different, although it makes some sense, it is in no way different from the religions who claim to have more than one God, believing in polytheism. For example, we all know that the Hindu religion has got many gods. Each of them has a specific function to fulfill. They are namely god of creation, god of protection, and god of destruction, just to name a few. They also claim that because they are functionally different, we call each of them as a separate god fulfilling the specific functions allotted to them. What difference does it make? How could you explain to them the Trinity in the way we claim and believe and convince them? It is just impossible. You cannot say that it is what it is, and you have to believe it—take it or leave it! They will only laugh at it and never going to understand the Trinity and believe one God existing in *three persons*. Well, in my understanding, even two-third of Christians do not understand the Trinity and believe it but accept and believe it because that is how they have been taught, or that is the faith they have been following for many generations.

Again, we should have an open mind to understand the Trinity the way Scriptures talk about it! Just consider the following way to understand the Trinity.

Father: the *only* sovereign God.

Jesus (Word): the Son of God.

Holy Spirit: the Spirit of God.

Does it mean one is greater or lower than the other? *Not at all!*

They don't even think that they in any means claim superiority over the other, nor consider one is lower than the other! They exist in such a unity and harmony as though they are *one*. This does not endorse the world view that they exist as "one in three and three in one."

Neither can we say otherwise like they exist something like twins or triplets! Identical but different!

We all know that they are all existing, and there is no doubt it!

There is one more problem. When a preacher addresses God, thinking within himself that he means to address the Father, the congregation may not understand that he addresses the Father, they might even think that he is addressing Jesus, the Son of God. Sometimes vice versa! This again does not endorse the world view of "one in three and three in one." When you say they are functionally different, you have to address any one of them accordingly!

For example, let us consider prayer!

When Jesus taught His disciples how to pray, He told them to address the prayer to the Father in heaven (Matthew 6:9). He has also told them to ask the Father in His (Jesus) name. The Scriptures also indicate that the Holy Spirit of God helps us to pray (Romans 8:26). If the Trinity means according to what we have understood and believe that they exist "one in three and three in one," how do we address the prayer, and to whom should we address the prayer? Should we address the prayer to the Father or to the Son or to the Holy Spirit? We could address the prayer to God (using this term); any one of them would hear it and any one of them would answer it. When Jesus taught us to pray, He used a pattern which is the right way of doing it. Again, when the early Pentecostals started to pray only to Jesus, they believe God is one, and now He has revealed Himself in and through Jesus Christ according to the Scriptures (John 1:18). They claimed that whether to pray to the Father or to Jesus, it just means the same. They are also not wrong because the Scriptures endorses it. If we believe Trinity in the above ideology, that is in a way correct too. But over the years, they have been blamed for it and branded as Jesus-only group; they don't believe in Trinity, and they are wrong.

Jehovah's Witnesses are another big problem. They acknowledge only Jehovah as God and never accept Trinity nor acknowledge Jesus as God at all. They don't even acknowledge Jesus as Savior. Not even as the Son of God, but only a prophet (now it appears they are accepting Jesus as the Son of God but not the Savior). According to what they claim, there is no salvation through or by Jesus, and they believe that only Jehovah saves, ignoring what Jesus Christ has done for salvation.

The whole world, besides Judaic Christians, Catholics, Protestants, and other believers, including Pentecostals, claim that all those who call themselves Christians also worship three gods, namely the Father, the Son, and the Holy Spirit. They neither understand Trinity nor accept Trinity and call them as liars because we say we believe in monotheism but worship three gods. We have no rights to blame them because we cannot properly explain and prove it to them the way we believe Trinity.

So a clear understanding about Trinity is necessary in order to strongly root it in our faith and properly explain to those who ask you questions about Trinity. First, we have to understand it clearly, and then we can talk or explain what we believe in. It has gone so deep into our minds that Trinity means *one* in *three* and *three* in *one*.

Let us consider the following scriptures:

John 1:18 says that no man has seen God at any time, the only begotten Son, who was in the bosom of the Father has declared Him (revealed Him). John 1:1 says that the Son was the Word in the beginning who was with God and was the brightness of His (the Father's) glory and the express image of the Father (Hebrews 1:4). But there was an exception. The first created man (Adam) and woman (Eve) had seen God and were communicating with Him directly. This was exception because they had not fallen into sin yet. Since the day they fell into sin, a veil fell between God and mankind, and the sovereign God and God became invisible to the naked eyes of man.

Jesus, who was the Word of God at that time, became flesh (John 1:12) and dwelt among men. Jesus, who although being in the form of God did not consider it to be worthy to call Himself equal with God, took the form of a man and humbled Himself even to the death on the cross (Philippians 2:5–8). This does not mean that He is inferior to the Father. Jesus also said, "He that has seen me hath seen the Father, because He is the intrinsic image of the Father" (John 14:9, Hebrews 1:4).

When the disciples asked Him, "Show us the Father," Jesus answered and said to them, "You don't believe that I am in my Father and my Father is in me? [John 14:9–11]. It is a figurative expression that although we are two distinct person, we are one and the same. I look like Him because I am His only begotten Son, and that is why I said if you had seen me, you have seen the Father. My thinking is exactly the same as the Father thinks. I do all the works just exactly like my Father if He had been here Himself." Just think of the terminology which was used to describe the marriage relationship between a man and a woman. Jesus said, "The man shall leave the father and mother and cleave to his wife, and they twain shall be one flesh" (Matthew 19:5). They are still two distinct persons, but because they are united in marriage, they are *one flesh*. But they are going to live separately as a man and a woman for the rest of their life, even into eternity. This is a figurative expression.

Let us consider our relationship with Christ.

In Colossians 1:27, we read, "Christ in you is the hope of glory."

WHO RULES THE WORLD, GOD OR SATAN?

In 2 Corinthians 5:17, we read, "If any man be in Christ, he is a new creature. Old things are passed away. Behold, everything becomes *new*." We find two different expressions given here. One is "if we are in Christ," and the other is "if Christ is in us." What does it convey, and what do we understand by these expressions? Do both the expressions mean the same or different? To get the meaning correctly, we have to go to Ephesians 3:17: "That Christ may dwell in our hearts by FAITH. It is by Faith we know Christ is dwelling in our hearts." Physically? No. He has also promised that He will be with us all the time. Physically? No. By faith, and Jesus Christ honors our faith according to His promise in Matthew 28:20.

The Scriptures also describe another kind of relationship with the Holy Spirit—the Spirit of God (John 14:17). Even the Spirit of Truth, who is also the Holy Spirit, will come and dwell with you and shall be in you. It could mean in two ways. Jesus said, "I am with you always even to the end of the world" (Matthew 28:20). After saying these words, the Scripture confirms that He ascended to heaven and seated on the right hand of God until the day appointed for Him to come back to earth for the millennial rule over the earth. But the Holy Spirit, on the other hand, was sent to the earth on the day of Pentecost with a commission to dwell with and in the believers until Jesus returns to the earth.

To understand all these, we have to first understand the dispensational functioning of the Father, Jesus, the Son of God, and the Holy Spirit, the Spirit of God.

I will give a short introduction to that in this chapter and give a vivid explanation in the next chapters. So please follow these articles every month and read them carefully.

The dispensation of the Father from the creation of mankind until Jesus came to the earth amounted to roughly four thousand years. The dispensation of Jesus Christ, the Son of God, spread over a period of thirty-three and a half years. The dispensation of the Holy Spirit, the Spirit of God (the present dispensation we are living in) spread approximately over two thousand years until Jesus returns back to the earth. The final dispensation of Jesus Christ is otherwise called the millennial rule (one thousand years) of Jesus on the earth before the final white throne judgment. If we understand the events in the chronological order according to the Scriptures, we will be able to understand Trinity in the Godhead. May the Spirit of God lead you and help you!

The Necessity for Three Different Expressions of Godhead

The sovereign God, who is the controller of the entire universe and the matters thereof, has many different sections or departments to manage their smooth running and operations. For many, it may look a different concept or approach. But in my opinion, it will answer many questions about the Trinity. We may argue that God is omnipotent (almighty), omniscient (all-knowing), omnipresent (present all over), and so on, and why does He need assistance to rule the entire Universe? Just think of the angels namely Michael, Gabriel, Lucifer, cherubim, and twenty-four elders described in the Scriptures. Why should God need them? They are all created living beings. God is Almighty, but He needs these members to assist Him in His whole operations. If He does not need them, they would never have been created. The Scriptures has a lot to tell about them, such as the need for their existence. Can we question God, "Why do you need all of them?" Can't He just speak and everything will happen the way He wants and every living and nonliving things would simply obey Him? Then why? Where do the Son of God and the Holy Spirit of God come in, and why have they been distinctly recognized in the Godhead. Is it not interesting? Let us find answers for all these questions in the Scriptures!

CHAPTER 7

Who Is the Father?

We will start analyzing the *names* of God as revealed in the Scriptures.

1. God or Elohim: *Elohim is the only name of God* revealed in the book of Genesis. This also reveals from time immemorial how the universe was in existence until He brought everything into order by His Word (later revealed as Jesus) and found them to be very good. In Hebrew, Elohim is a plural noun. This is referred to in Genesis repeatedly both in singular and in plural. "There is no God beside me; I am God and there is none else." It also says, "Let us make man in our image, after our likeness." And again it says, "Man has become like *one of us*." And again in Babel, it says, "Let us go down and confound their language." And again in a vision to Isaiah, it says, "Whom shall I send and who will go for us?" Let us study all these one by one.
2. Lord or Jehovah: Jehovah is the expression of God's being. It also expresses the embodiment of *perfect love and perfect truth*, which is more fully expressed in Jesus. When the first time he revealed Himself by a name to Moses, He said "I AM THAT I AM." The name Jehovah is used by some translators for the name of the covenant God of Israel (Exodus 6:3), which also means The Lord, who is holy, righteous and full

of love and truth. We later find the *love* and *truth* is revealed in Jesus Christ. *Mercy (grace)* and *truth* are met together; *righteousness and peace* have kissed each other. Truth (Jesus) shall spring out of the earth, and *righteousness* (Jehovah) shall look down from heaven (Psalm 85:11–12). The very first day He created man, He subjected him under the law (Genesis 2:17). We read, "He commanded him." Can we forget here the apostle saying, "The law is not made for a righteous man"? (1 Timothy 1:9). Righteousness ranks top in God's nature and characters.

3. God Almighty or El Shaddai: This character is often misunderstood. Almightiness does not mean that He can do everything and anything. Scripture also says that He *cannot* lie (Titus 1:2). Because He cannot lie, does that mean He is not Almighty? Not at all! Almighty means that He can do all things within His *nature* and *character*. He cannot do anything because He is the *source* of everything. The name El Shaddai reveals this capability. Mainly, He is the source of *life*, *love*, and *blessings* to all His creatures. He breathed into Adam, and he became a living soul (Genesis 2:7). God so loved the world that He gave His only begotten Son, Jesus Christ, to the world to die on our behalf so that we might live on His terms (John 3:16). The thought expressed in the name Shaddai is different. It means "breasted," meaning all-bountifulness in the divine sense, which is the *pourer* and *shedder forth* of all blessings *temporal* and *spiritual*.

4. The Most High God (the highest): This appears fifty-three times in the Scriptures. Totally sovereign, unparalleled, incomparable. It also means there is no one equal or no one above Him. Even Melchizedek, who has no genealogy but called as King of Righteousness and Peace, is only recognized as the priest of the Most High God (Hebrews 7:3). When Lucifer wanted to exalt himself, he could only think that he will be like the Most High (Isaiah 14:14). But anyway, he was cast down to earth and later to hell.

About Jesus, Paul declared, "Who being in the *form of* God thought it not robbery to be *equal* with God, humbled Himself to take the likeness of men" (Philippians 2:6). Jesus and the Holy Spirit are neither parallel nor equal with the Most High God.

5. Lord or Adonai: The name Adonai or Lord teaches that a relationship answering to that of servants to their lord (master) and of wives to their husbands exists between God in heaven and His creature man on the earth. This relationship also declares the dependence on Him and faithfulness toward Him. Because He is their rightful Lord, He is bound to sustain, keep, and help them. More so, the church is church because it acknowledges this relationship, and the world is world because it denies this relationship. The psalmist (David) acknowledges and repeats this language throughout the Psalms. "O LORD our Lord, how excellent is Thy Name in all the earth" (Psalm 148:13). "O LORD our Lord, has put all things under his feet" (Psalm 8:6). It recognizes God as his Master (Adonai).

6. The Everlasting God or El Olam: The sovereign God is from everlasting to everlasting. To Moses, He said "I AM THAT I AM" (Exodus 3:14). He is Alpha and Omega, the beginning and the end. His beginning and His end is hidden from knowledge and understanding of mankind. He is self-existent from time immemorial. No man can fathom the beginning of God's existence and also the end of the eternity. We have to wait to know all these secrets hidden from mankind until we go to heaven.

7. Father, Son, and the Holy Ghost: Here is where the Trinity is actually revealed. Until the end of the Old Testament, Trinity was *not* revealed in any form to mankind. One of the old renowned theologian said, "The New Testament lies hid in the Old, and the Old is opened in the New." It is only when Jesus Himself revealed this great mystery when He told His disciples to baptize them who believe in His name for their salvation "in the name of the Father, of the

Son, and of the Holy Ghost." He didn't say "in the *names* of the Father, the Son, and the Holy Ghost." So then, the name of the Father and of the Son and of the Holy Ghost is one name, not three or many.

Trinity as Revealed in Their Dispensational Activities

In order to understand the Trinity more clearly, we have to understand God's three dispensations. Many people are not even familiar with this terminology. The total number of seven thousand years determined by God for mankind can be divided in *three* major dispensations.

1. The dispensation of the Father—four thousand years.
2. The dispensation of Jesus Christ, the Son of God whose one thousand years (yet to come) of rule (millennial) over the earth is going to start after His second coming. (This one thousand years *may or may not* include the thirty-three and a half years. He lived on the face of this Earth.)
3. The dispensation of the Holy Spirit—two thousand years (approx.) from the conception of Jesus in the womb of the Virgin Mary until the day of the coming of the Lord and the beginning of the millennium.

To understand all these, we have to study and learn the three different dispensations—namely the dispensation of the Father, the dispensation of the Son, and the dispensation of the Holy Spirit. Please read the following very carefully to understand the doctrine of Trinity very clearly. Let the Spirit of God help you to understand this.

First Dispensation: The Dispensation of the Father

These three dispensation are classified only for own understanding of the Trinity, but all of them are still working according to their individual responsibilities. For example, Father is the *author* of all creations both in heaven and on earth and beneath the earth, everything that exists, including mankind. But He did not create all things by Himself.

If we read John 1–3, in the beginning was the Word (Jesus), and the Word was *with* God, and the Word was God. The same was in the beginning with God (Father). All things were made by Him and without Him (Jesus) nothing was made that was made.

If we read Colossians 1:15–16, Jesus is the image of the invisible God, the firstborn of every creature, for by Him (Jesus) all things that are in heaven and earth, visible and invisible, whether they be thrones or dominions or principalities or powers, were created. All things were created by Him (Jesus) and for Him.

If we read Hebrews 1:2, in these last days, God has spoken unto us by His Son (Jesus), whom He hath appointed heir of all things by whom He (Jesus) made the worlds.

If we read Ephesians 3:9, we are able to understand that God who created all things by Jesus Christ had hidden these things as a mystery from the beginning of the world.

The whole act of creation looks like a *mystery*. God is self-existent. Where was Jesus, and how did He play the role in the creation activities. If *both* are one and the same, how would you explain the four quotations I have given above?

It is quite obvious, and both Father and the Son were involved in the matter of creation. But throughout the period of the Old Testament until Jesus came and revealed Himself as the Son of God in the intrinsic (express) image of the Father (Hebrews 1:4), Jesus Christ appears to be silent. In fact, the Father was fully operational over everything He had created both in heaven and on earth. Where was Jesus? He was appearing occasionally. He stood in the wilderness as the Rock from which God provided water to the people of Israel. Through Moses, all the people of Israel drank from the spiritual mountain in the wilderness, who was Jesus Christ (1 Corinthians 10:4).

In another occasion, when the three Hebrew children were persecuted in the burning furnace, Jesus appeared as the Son of God along with them to protect and to save them. The King Nebuchadnezzar exclaimed before all the people gathered there that "I see four men walking in the midst of the fire, and the likeness of the fourth man was like the Son of God" (Daniel 3:25). Obviously, it could be no other than Jesus Christ.

At the same time, Jesus Christ is directly or indirectly revealed in *every book* of the Bible. This is another mystery in the Godhead. I have written another series of articles under the title "Jesus Christ in Every Book of the Bible," which reveals wonderfully the reflection of the presence of Jesus Christ throughout the history of the Old Testament.

It was the Father who dealt with everyone and everything. King David, who was the anointed king over Israel, was given to understand this great mystery of the Godhead or the Trinity. But he did not expressly reveal it to everyone even through his psalms. Here I am giving some of those revelations for our understanding. In Psalm 22, he reveals the existence of Jesus Christ as his Lord and prophetically describes His cry at the time of His death on the cross of Calvary (Psalm 22:1). In Psalm 23, he recognizes him (Jesus) as his shepherd. In Psalm 24, he exalts Him (Jesus) as the King of Glory and so on. This does not give an understanding that both God the Father and Jesus Christ are one and the same. Don't get confused.

All the prophets starting from Moses to Malachi was dealt with by the Father only. Maybe Jesus was an observer throughout these ages. Prophets Isaiah, Zachariah, and Malachi were prophesying about Jesus Christ as the coming Messiah and the savior of the world and not as an instrument of leading, guiding, or governing them or their activities. Jesus all through these years of dispensation is a silent observer waiting for His turn to come as the Messiah to this world and offer Himself as the sacrifice for all mankind for the remission of their sins.

So then, now where is the Father, and what is He doing? Strange question to ask. It is, indeed! Let us try to find out and understand it. He is definitely seated on the *throne* in heaven. He is probably overseeing everything, having His only begotten Son Jesus Christ seated on the *throne* on His right-hand side. Jesus is exalted above everything and everybody, even in heaven. I would say the Father is proud of the Son, and the Son is proud of the Father. What a wonderful scene to visualize! He is just waiting for the *right time* to ask the son to go and proceed with His *final judgement*!

The Revelation of Jesus Christ as the Messiah

The revelation of Jesus Christ approximately two thousand years ago and the time (thirty-three and a half years) He spent on the face of the earth to fulfill the plan, purpose, and the command of the Father cannot be classified or divided as part of the dispensation of the Son of God. This period could safely be included in the "dispensation of the Holy Spirit," which we are going to study and consider next. Jesus came to fulfill the plan of God.

- To seek and save the lost (John 18:11).
- To reconcile mankind back to the Father duly and properly.
- To defeat and destroy the work of Satan, who is still the prince of this world (1 John 3:8).
- To establish the eternal kingdom of God on earth.
- To deliver the captives free.
- To remove the sin and curse from mankind and from the earth totally.

All these demands of the Father in Jesus Christ was meticulously fulfilled by Him without any fault of flaw. And He was lifted up and exalted above all the creatures of heaven and of the world (Philippians 2:9) and was offered the magnificent and glorious throne on the right hand of the Father. This had to happen in the middle of human history. That is why the human history is divided as "before Christ" and "after Christ." This demarcation is necessary to understand the role of the Son of God.

CHAPTER 8

Who Is the Holy Spirit?

Who Is the Holy Spirit and What Is His Identity?

Most often He is recognized and referred to as the third person in Trinity. There is nothing like that in the Scriptures. It is purely an assumption of the theologians and Bible scholars. By telling like this, they are bringing in more confusion. Holy Spirit is often referred to as Spirit of God (Genesis 1:2; Isaiah 48:16, 61:1; Zechariah 12:10) and the Spirit of Christ (Romans 8:9, 1 Peter 1:11) and the Holy Spirit. So what is His personality? By simply saying He is the third person of the Trinity makes no sense! Does He have any image or likeness? No. Does He have a personality? Yes! He is not a thing but a person. How do we identify a personality? Not just by the physical form, because none of the angelic and spirit beings have a physical body. But they do have a spiritual recognizable form or a body! That does not indicate that they have a personality. Personality is characterized by the presence of the following faculties: (1) mind (thinking), (2) seeing (eyes), (3) hearing (ears), (4) feeling (emotions), (5) will (makes decisions, called the freewill, ability to make choices), and (6) ability to make decisions and to bring them to pass. We have all these faculties working in us through our physical body. That is why we are called as a person.

The Holy Spirit is also a person and not simply a Spirit only!

1. He has (knows) the mind of God. (1 Corinthians 2:11)
2. He can see and has the capacity to oversee us. (Romans 8:14)
3. He hears our prayers and communicate the same to the Father. (Romans 8:26)
4. He feels. Grieve not the Holy Spirit. (Ephesians 4:30)
5. He will not strive with men always. (Genesis 6:3)
6. He has the same will as of the Father. (Isaiah 48:16)
7. He makes decisions according to the will of the Father and of the Son and communicates to us and also executes them in and through us. (John 16:13, the entire Acts of the Apostles, otherwise called the Acts of the Holy Ghost)
8. He is the source of supernatural power.

Ye shall receive power when the Holy Ghost comes upon you (Acts 1:8). He acts independently but not indifferently. He executes what the Father of the Son thinks or wills. There is an absolute harmony between them. He doesn't need to take orders neither from the Father nor from the son because He knows their mind and will. The Father sent the Son to be born as a man, live as a man, die as a man, but was raised from the dead to be the first fruit of resurrection. The same Father sent the Holy Spirit on the day of Pentecost to empower the disciples to carry on the ministry Jesus has commissioned to them. He will be working in this world until the rapture of the church and the day of the Lord! Then He will be taken up to the heavens, and the Son will descend and rule this world for one thousand years, otherwise called the millennial rule of Jesus Christ in this world.

Second Dispensation: The Dispensation of the Holy Spirit

It might surprise many readers because this was not normally used or preached in many churches, spiritual platforms, or even in theological and church pulpits. If I say that this dispensation starts from the day of conception of Jesus Christ, our Lord, to the day of the Lord, including the rapture, could anyone dispute it? Holy Spirit was given the total responsibility to cause the birth of the church from the day of Pentecost, protecting the church against all odds and evils from all satanic attacks, influence, and acts of deceiving the believers who constitute the body of Christ. God is still on the throne. Jesus Christ is on the right hand of God on His own throne waiting for the green signal from the father to *return* to the earth and do justice and rule the earth by the rod of iron with justice and peace. The Holy Spirit is in action since the day of Pentecost until *today* and will be acting until the rapture of the church.

He began His work from day one of the conception of Jesus in womb of the Virgin Mary. He protected Him (Jesus) from the wrath of Herod, from all dangers which could have been caused by Satan. He brought to His remembrance (John 14:26) the words of Moses and of the prophets and helped Him to have strong and wise conversations with Pharisees and Sadducees in the synagogues and so on. Jesus had to be kept pure and holy until He fulfils the greatest commission of taking on Himself the death on the cross (Hebrews 9:14). Because Jesus was born of a woman with all passions of any human being, He needs divine protection to be totally sinless. The Bibles suggests He (Jesus) knew no sin at all. It was because of the presence of the Holy Spirit, His protection, His guidance, His leading, His power to resist all evil and to escape whenever needed not to fall prey in to the wiles of the devil. Oh! What a great responsibility He had to be with Jesus, who is in His human form to protect Him (Jesus) from all the devices of the devil, who was trying to stop Jesus from going to the cross. He counseled Him, comforted Him, strengthened Him, and protected Him all through His life on the earth.

Holy Spirit was with Jesus all the way like an invisible companion watching over Him (Jesus) all the time. Because of that, Satan had a tough time to go near Jesus. He was the greatest protector known according to the Scriptures. Jesus was always sensitive of His (Holy Spirit) presence with Him. He was always attentive to the leading and guidance of the Holy Spirit, which oftentimes we are not. He was His counselor at the marriage function in Cana of Galilee and led Him to perform the first miracle (John 2:1–10). He never let Him down under any circumstance.

According to the plan of God, He (the Holy Spirit) descended on Him visibly and anointed Him when He came out of the waters after being baptized by John (Luke 3:22). From then onward, He took care of His ministry. To begin with, He (the Holy Spirit) led Him in to the wilderness to be tempted by the devil in order to strengthen Him spiritually (Matthew 4:1–10), to enable Him to resist the temptations the devil might bring into His life later on.

After some time on a Sabbath day, He went into the synagogue and started to read from the book of Isaiah these words: "The Spirit of the Lord is upon Me (Jesus) because He hath anointed me to preach the gospel, to deliver the people from all kinds of bondage, and to preach the acceptable year of the Lord" (Luke 4:16–19). The Holy Spirit brought to His remembrance the words spoken by Isaiah.

We also read in Acts 10:38 that God was *anointed* with the Holy Ghost and with *power*, and He (Jesus) went about doing good and healing all who were oppressed of the devil, for God was with Him. These are clear indications that the Holy Spirit played a major role in the earthly life of Jesus Christ. Their individual dispensation and function makes each of them different. The Holy Spirit strengthened Jesus when He was going through the agony of suffering and even to death on the cross. Jesus died and was buried.

According to the plan of God, three days after the death of Jesus, in order to fulfill the Scriptures, the Holy Spirit brought Him out in to life bodily. Romans 8:11 reads, "If the Holy Spirit of Him [God] that raised up Jesus from the dead dwell in you, He [Holy Spirit] that raised up Christ from the dead shall also quicken your *mortal* bodies by His Spirit that dwells in you." This is very important for us to know that the body of Jesus was not left behind. It was transformed in to a glorious spiritual body in the same likeness as he was while he was living on the face of the earth. We have to compare this to the transformation which is going to take place at the time of rapture. Those who are alive at the time of rapture has to be transformed from this living mortal body into immortal glorious body like what Jesus has now we need the Holy Spirit. According to the Scripture we just read, our mortal bodies cannot be transformed as magic into immortal glorious body. You should have been anointed (filled or baptized) by the Holy Spirit in order to be transformed in to that glorious body in a twinkling of an eye and be taken away without seeing or tasting the death. What a wonderful privilege!

The work of the Holy Spirit continues. He came upon all the 120 including His (Jesus) own disciples on the day of Pentecost (Acts 2:1–5). They began to preach and deliver the people from the bondage of sin, sickness, and Satan. This started happening by and through the disciples. The church was born, which is also referred to as the body of Christ. The church is going on surviving against all odds and persecutions and growing and spreading all over the world, although it is still one body of Christ (the universal church irrespective of denominations). The ministry is still not over. The Holy Spirit is still working with the people of God until Jesus comes.

The Holy Spirit is now working with the church, and all believers round the globe is restraining the appearance of the antichrist. If we read 2 Thessalonians 2:6–7, we come across a restrainer or a hinderer who is now working on the earth and is stopping the appearance of the antichrist. Who could that be? It is the Holy Spirit working along with the church that is doing it because He (Holy Spirit) could be the only person who has the power and authority to do so. His dispensation ends at the rapture and the appearance of the antichrist, followed by the tribulation period, followed by the open appearance of Jesus Christ, who is the ruler of the next dispensation of the Son of God for a thousand years.

CHAPTER 9

Who Is Jesus Christ?

The Dispensation of the Son Of God, Jesus Christ

This is the most important dispensational section in understanding the Trinity. Jesus Christ, the Son of God, played a major role in creation, the most important role in the redemption, restoration, and reconciliation of mankind back to God from the fallen and lost condition since Adam fell into *sin* and was separated from God the Father. Satan's dominance over mankind (humanity) was unspeakable and was increasing day by day. Within some 1,600 years from Adam, Satan has caused humanity to be totally corrupt and sinful. God saw the *wickedness* of man was *great* in the earth and that the very imagination of the thoughts of his heart is *only evil continually* (Genesis 6:5). Satan was successful enough to make the minds of mankind totally corrupt and evil within about 1,600 years of man's life on the face of the earth. God could not tolerate evil growing and increasing day by day; He decided to destroy the entire living creatures and saved only Noah and his family to let His creation continue to live on the earth. He brought the destruction by flood on the earth. But the humanity continued on the earth.

After some 2,400 years (a total of four thousand years approximately from Adam), Jesus Christ, the Son of God, came and interrupted the history of mankind according to the plan of God and did what He had to do to restore the situation. In spite of God's disappointment over mankind, He still loved the world, and He gave His only begotten Son that whosoever believes in Him (Jesus Christ) should not perish but have everlasting life (John 3:16). This was a great blow for Satan. He knew that he is going to lose his dominion over mankind because of Jesus. He knows that he has lost it already.

Something very important took place during this time which the Jehovah's Witnesses fail to recognize. When Jesus Christ went up the top of the mountain of transfiguration, something very important took place. When Moses and Elijah appeared along with Jesus, there came a voice from the clouds that said, "This is my beloved Son [Jesus] in whom I am well pleased; hear ye Him [Jesus]" (Matthew 17:5). These are the last words of the Father (Jehovah) spoken to be heard of men. After this, the Father never spoke any word until today or even until the end of the world. Why? The Father has committed all judgments to his Son, Jesus (John 5:22), and exalted Jesus above every other creations both in heaven and on earth and beneath the earth. God has highly exalted Him and has given a name above every name (Philippians 2:9). God has crowned Him with *glory* and set Him over the work of his hands and has put all things under His feet. For in that He put *all* in *subjection* under Him (Hebrews 2:7–10). The Jehovah's Witnesses don't want to accept this and keep rejecting Jesus as the *only way* for salvation of mankind.

This changed the course of the history of humanity. But He (Jesus) died, rose again from the dead, and ascended to heaven to be seated on the right hand of God, the Father. Then the dispensation of the Holy Spirit began. It was by the request (prayer) of Jesus Christ the Holy Spirit was given to the earth to anoint, empower, guide, lead, protect, and warn the children of God and also the world through the servants of God and so on. By the anointing of the Holy Spirit, the *church* was ushered in. (Born as we see from the day of Pentecost). We are now in the close of the dispensation of the Holy Spirit. The coming of the Lord is sooner than ever. Almost all the signs of the end times are being fulfilled. At the secret coming of the Lord, the church will be *raptured* and will be taken away. The Holy Spirit also will be taken away from the world as His dispensation is over. The restrainer (the Holy Spirit and the church) will be also gone. Then the antichrist will be revealed (2 Thessalonians 2:7). Then from the day of the Lord, the final dispensation of the Son of God (Jesus Christ) will begin and continue for one thousand years.

How Do We Interpret the Trinity in the Light of the Above Facts?

God: The Father and the only sovereign God, self-existent, Alpha and Omega the beginning and the end, controls everything that exists and lives forever and ever. There is none like Him, no one equal to Him and no one greater than Him. Forever He is Jehovah, the only sovereign God!

Jesus: The son of God and not the same as god. He is the replica or the express (intrinsic) image of God (Hebrews 1:4). He knows the *mind* of God, imitates everything as God, performs everything as God Himself. But He was the Son of God, He is the Son of God, and He will be the Son of God forever into all eternity. He is going to judge everything and everybody in heaven, earth, and below the earth. He is exalted over everything in heaven, on earth, and beneath the earth. Before Him every knee shall bow, and every tongue will confess that He is Lord. Is He equal with God? No! Is He greater than God? No! Is He lower than God? No! That is why He is recognized as part of Trinity!

Holy Spirit: the Spirit of God is not the same as God. He does not have form or image like Jesus, but He does have all the faculties of a person. He will not imitate God like Jesus, but He will perform everything as God or as though God was present Himself. He knows the mind of God as well as Jesus. He reveals the will of God to men. He teaches men. He guides men. He keeps men from falling away into sin and into the wiles of the devil. He anoints men. He empowers men to perform *supernatural things*. He operates the gifts of the Spirit through men by faith. He glorifies Jesus at all times and in turn bring glory to God. He is a silent, invisible operator and performer of God's will and activities. He is the author of the written Word of God. He initiates the act of salvation in anybody's life. He transforms our mortal bodies into glorified bodies at the time of rapture as he did to Jesus in His resurrection. He will never seek glory for Himself. Is He equal with God? No! Is He greater than God? No! Is He lower than God? No! That is why He is recognized as part of Trinity! Forever He is the Spirit of God.

Their Existence

All of them exist from the very beginning: They are self-existent. There is no record anywhere in the Scriptures that any of them (Son and the Holy Spirit) was created. All the other heavenly beings, including archangels, angels, etc., were all created beings. "In the beginning was the Word, and the Word was with God and the Word was God" (John 1:1). If we read it very carefully, it reveals something which we normally don't pay attention. We all know very definitely that the Word refers to Jesus. The narration starts with "In the beginning was the Word," as though the Word was preexisting before God. It didn't say "In the beginning was God," and the Word was with God. The relationship between God and Jesus is described as Father and Son. John 17:21 reads, "That they may be one as you Father are in Me and I in you that they may also be one with us." Jesus says here that "Father, You and I are *one* although we are existing in two different persons." Let us read what Paul says in Hebrews 1:3–4: "God in the last days [since when? I will let you know shortly] spoken unto us by His Son [Jesus], whom He appointed heir of all things by whom also He made the worlds, who being the brightness of His Glory and the express image of His person and upholding all things by the word of His power." You want to know since when? Let us read Matthew: 17:5. In the mountain of transfiguration, God spoke from the clouds, "This is my beloved Son in whom I am well pleased; hear ye Him!" After that time, the Father God never spoke nor revealed Himself to anyone. There is no need any more to reveal Himself. Even the book of Revelation is completely the revelation of Jesus Christ.

John 1:18 says very clearly, "No man has seen God at any time, the only begotten Son, who is [not was] in the bosom of the Father has declared [revealed] Him." Jesus, who is the express (intrinsic) image of the Father, has now been revealed in the place of Father God

Himself for doing everything which the Father would have done if He had been here Himself. The invisible God has become visible in and through Christ.

How Did Jesus Identify the Father When He Was in This World?

This is very important to understand the Trinity.

1. He (Jesus) always addresses Him as Father (John 11:41–42) (Luke 23:46).
2. He always identifies Himself as the Son sent in to this world (Isaiah 61:1).
3. He said He was sent by the father (John 3:16).
4. He said My Father is greater than I (John 14:28).
5. He said My Father works in and through me (John 10, 25, 37–38).
6. He said, "I came to do and fulfil the Will of the Father only" (Luke 22:42).
7. He said, "Ask my Father in My Name." (John 14:13–14; 16:23).
8. He called Him as His Father and Lord of heaven and earth (Matthew 11:28, Luke 10:21).
9. He called Him as righteous Father (John 17:25).
10. He said, "Always My Father testifies about Me, glorifies Me, and glorifies Himself in Me."

Totally, Jesus mentioned in all the four gospels put together about the Father 176 times and not in one instance He identified Himself with the Father or equal to Him.

Jesus always kept Himself as the one who was sent by the Father to *reveal* the identity of God by works and fulfilling the will of the Father. The Father had given Him a commission that He (Jesus) should die the cursed death on the cross to reconcile the lost mankind to Himself. God, being sovereign, cannot offer Himself as a sacrifice He has to send His only begotten Son to fulfill that job. He is

God *of all things in heaven and earth*. Jesus Christ has been given the authority over all things of heaven and earth. The Father is delighted over the Son about that. He is the revelation of the Father and not a dual personality—sometimes as Father and some other times as the Son. Hence, the term "one in three and three in one" makes no sense at all. That is not the correct method of characterizing Trinity. Jesus is always the Son of God into all eternity. He has been assigned the position on the throne on the right hand of God forever. He is never going to displace the Father for eternity! He has been exalted over all the creatures in heaven, including the archangels and other angels. We don't have to analyze who is greater among them. It will be foolish to do so. For all our understanding purposes, they are equal in exercising authority and power over everything in the universe, including the spiritual realms and the demonic kingdom. But still He is the Son.

This is how Trinity exists. Amen!

CHAPTER 10

Jesus versus Satan!

It is high time that we pay serious attention to this most neglected subject. Who is Jesus, and who is Satan? Many Christian theologians, religious leaders, and even the anti-Christians do not want to phrase it together because they think that Jesus Christ cannot be compared equally to Satan. But I am not convinced whether they truly believe what they say about Jesus Christ or they say but don't believe what they say! In my opinion, only their lips confess like that, but in their mind, they fully believe that Jesus is powerless before satanic power and influence over mankind. They will even proclaim to the world that it is blasphemy! Dear readers, be honest about what you are thinking about this subtitle.

The Battle between Satan and Jesus

It all started right from the Garden of Eden. The Garden of Eden was the nicest place mankind would love to live in. Peace and communion with God were present. No fear, no anxiety, no hardships, no suffering. What a wonderful place it should have been! The only tragedy was Satan had permission to access the Garden of Eden. Many theologians give various interpretations that Adam and Eve was in a perfect sinless situation until they disobeyed God's command and ate the forbidden fruit. Actually, this statement is very incorrect. Both of them were in a state of innocence but not in the sinless perfect situation. Maybe it was a sinless situation but not a perfect situation because Satan, the source of all sins, was present there already! And there were no protection given to them by any means either by a hedge or a wall of protection, like how Job was protected. Neither the blood of Jesus, which was available to them like how it is available for the protection to all believers who believes in His name. They were exposed to sin. Satan, knowing this, seized this opportunity to deceive them, and he was successful. As a result of this, Adam lost the dominion, and Satan took dominion over all mankind. But he could not take dominion over the rest of the earth totally. Mankind became slave to the satanic rulership. Since the time mankind became slaves to Satan, they were no longer under the rulership of God whatsoever. God knows about this, Satan knows about it, and man knows about it also. Consider the words God said to Satan in the Garden of Eden: "I will put enmity between you and the woman, and between your seed [all the generation to come] and her seed [Jesus], and he shall bruise your head, and you shall bruise his heel" (Genesis 3:15). Jesus, who at that time was only in the Word form (John 1:1–2), was brought into the picture, and Satan was fully aware of that.

Satan knew right from the Garden of Eden that Jesus is going to come to fix him. No man born in the flesh and in sin could defeat him in any way. For the purpose of understanding, man in the flesh *cannot* overcome Satan, who is in the Spirit form. Men who have strong will power may be able to manage to resist him to some extent but never could overcome him in the flesh totally. It cannot be considered as victory over satanic spirits. In the like manner, women are weaker vessels in the flesh and are easily overcome by satanic power and influence.

The day when Adam and Eve faced the temptation of Satan and yielded to it, they lost communion with God or His Spirit. He has then become a victim of all satanic influences. He could not resist anything the devil brought on his way. This accounts for the failure of Adam and Eve to resist the temptations brought to them namely the lust of the eyes, lust of the flesh, and the pride of life (Genesis 3:12). From Adam, except the few chosen ones of God, like Enoch, who walked with God, and Noah, who lived righteously in the sight of God, no other men could resist the devil and overcome him. God took Enoch from seeing death and spared only Noah and his family from being destroyed all living things from the earth by flood. Then again, the descendants of Noah also could not resist the temptations of the devil, and they could never overcome the satanic influences. Why? In the flesh, no one could fight the devil and overcome him. Thereafter, again, only a few chosen people like Abraham, Moses, Joshua, Gideon, Samuel, David, Daniel, and the prophets were able to resist the devil to some extent, and with the help of the Spirit of God, they were able to defeat him. This was possible for them because they believed God and in His might (Hebrews 11) and was willing to obey His commandments and statutes and walk in His ways wholeheartedly in spirit and mind like Caleb. God, who knows the hearts of men, protected them from the wiles of the devil and helped them by His Spirit to overcome the devil. Until Jesus came to die on the cross and defeat Satan once and for all, mankind was totally helpless and slaves under Satan.

How Satan Has Authority over World Systems!

Satan has extended his kingdom on earth. Satan dwells in the celestial realm (the second heaven) and rules the terrestrial world. Paul writes to Ephesians (2:2), "You were once walked to the course of this world and according to the prince of the power of the air [the midair or the second heaven], the spirit which now works in the children of disobedience." He is confirming it in Ephesians 6:10–18. Jesus confirmed it in John 12:31. Paul further goes on to say in 2 Corinthians 4:4, referring to Satan, that he is the god of this world. Satan rules the world systems by influencing businesses, social, political, religious activities of the majority of mankind, save the delivered true believers and true Christians who follow the Lord faithfully.

Satan rules the world by his subjects which are fallen angels, fallen men and women, and demons of various kinds (Matthew 25:41, Revelation 12:7–12, John 8:44, 1 John 3:8–10, James 2:19).

Satan is the head of some religions and is the leader of many religious affairs (2 Corinthians 11:14, Revelation 2:9, 3:9).

Satan's Privileges and Powers

He has some privileges and powers, the details of which I have narrated in the first chapter. They are only a few, but there is lot more. He brings in lawlessness by influencing the political, social, and religious systems of the world because the entire system is under his control and rulership. He is also an invisible spiritual being; we neither see him nor know about how he really operates. We just fall into his trap and become prey to his deceptions. Because he has access to the presence of God as he was doing prior to his fall, he is able to obtain permission to even tempt and destroy even the righteous people of God, like Job, Peter, and others. By influencing the mind, he can deceive even the child of God very easily. He can cause sicknesses, disease, physical and mental maladies in our bodies, and destroy harmony and peace in our lives (Luke 13:16, Acts 10:38). He can hinder answer to our prayers (Daniel 10:12–21) to disappoint us and develop dissatisfaction toward God. He is totally immoral and leads the entire human race into total immorality, which displeases God in every way. He could even possess humans and rule over them completely.

All these are possible because he is a spirit being. Mankind is made up of soul, spirit, and body. They are not totally spiritual beings. Although the soul and the spirit are inseparable spirit forms, they are dwelling in a body made up of flesh, which is a mortal thing. The body has a lot of mortal matters. The body can become diseased, suffer physically, suffer curses, pain, emotions like anger, lusts, etc. The Spirit is helpless to protect the body by itself because most of the time the spirit does what the body wants, and that is why we commit sin, but the body refuses to do what the spirit wants.

Satan has more capabilities and powers than man. Man has a lot of weaknesses bodily, and Satan is able to seize them to his advantage. Man by himself cannot overcome Satan directly because he is actually Satan's slave. Now the question arises who can possibly overcome Satan? As I was explaining earlier, some men with the help of the Holy Spirit (Spirit of God) were able to overcome Satan and defeat him. This privilege was not available to everyone and not at all times. So someone else has to gain victory over him and make that victory available for all men who believe it and exercise that privilege. So Jesus has to come and do that.

Because of sin, every man is the slave of Satan. Man by himself cannot get over his sinful nature and gain victory over sin at all. So many yogis, rishis (were there in India since 1100 BC), priests, and religious leaders tried this over a long period of time by so many means, and nobody was able to attain the state of overcoming sins and Satan by themselves. These attempts were taking place even before Jesus came into this world. But no one was ever successful. Buddha became a yogi in 500 BC and started teaching good morals, and by doing so, anyone could live a happy life. He never taught how to overcome sin and Satan. Later it became a religion, called Buddhism, but this religion never teaches about God.

Even a very famous muni called Vishwamitra, while he was still meditating to overcome sin, fell to the teasing of a woman named Sakunthala and committed sexual sin with her, and she gave birth to a child for him. Later, when she brought the child to him, he rejected both the mother and the child on the grounds that they were representation of hindrances to his religious pursuit.

Why Jesus, the Son of God, Alone Could Defeat Satan?

Until Jesus came, every effort man attempted to overcome sin ended up in failure. Moreover, *sin* is connected to man's soul and spirit and just not the body only. The body just manifests the desires of the soul and spirit, which is easily influenced by Satan. The Spirit of God can also influence the human spirit. The difference is that Satan influences to do all immoral activities, whereas the Spirit of God influences to do *moral activities only*. Man's mind *always choose* to perform immoral (wicked) acts and rarely choose to perform moral (righteous) acts. That corrupts the entire body, soul, and spirit of a man. Throughout the human history, men tried to overcome this, but they could not.

The second reason is that everyone who was born and living in sin cannot overcome sin, neither help anyone else to overcome sin. Because Satan is the father, master, source of sin, and would never let anyone escape from his bondage unless someone delivers him from his bondage. Who could possibly deliver man from such bondage? That has to be someone who is totally sinless (free from the very nature of sin) and has divine power (meaning one who possesses spiritual power and authority), as Satan is a spiritual being. This is why Jesus had to be born of a virgin by the Holy Spirit of God and not by the will of man. He knew no sin and never committed any sin, and hence, He was the only qualified Son of God to be able to defeat Satan and overcome his power and authorities.

Another reason is that man is just not the body only, but he has a spiritual portion, the soul and the spirit, which is otherwise called the *inner man*. This inner man, comprised of the soul and spirit, is immortal. There may be some people who might argue that nothing is immortal, everything is going to be destroyed (annihilated) when people die. On the contrary, almost all religions (except Jehovah's Witnesses) believe in the immortality of the soul and the spirit. Otherwise *none* of the religions would have lasted until today if they didn't have faith in the immortality of the soul and the spirit. Satan is a spiritual being and also immortal until the time he is going to be punished eternally. The question is, how can a mortal being overcome an immortal being? That is why Jesus had to be born as a mortal man in flesh and God allowed Him to suffer and die on the cross but raised Him up on the third day, defeating the power of Satan even on the body of man. The power of resurrection of Jesus Christ accounts for the defeat of the entire satanic power and authority. No other man could have possibly achieved this to overcome sin and deliver mankind from the bondage of Satan.

This gives us the real picture of why mankind needs deliverance from the bondage Satan. Well, we find that man, with all his physical, mental, spiritual, and emotional capabilities, could never overcome satanic power and authority. Satan has more power and capacity to overcome man and subdue him. He is someone who is more powerful than the human strength. Men are no match for him. Man's body is full of weaknesses, subject to sufferings, diseases, emotional weakness, and finally death. God did not create mankind to be in such a condition of life and never see eternity. God wanted man to have dominion over everything in this world. But now, alas! Everything is lost. The Bible declares that the life of a man is in the blood. "For the life of the flesh is in the blood" (Leviticus 17:11), so our life has some relationship to the blood and vice versa! As much as the sin has got something to do with the death (for the wages of sin is death, Romans 6:23) and death has got something to do with the life (death is defined as the loss of life) and life has got something to do with the blood (because the life of the flesh is in the blood), the blood has got something to do with the sins. That is the reason why the Bible declares there is no remission of sins without shedding of the blood. (Hebrews 9:22) God has set forth Jesus to be propitiation through faith in His blood, which was shed on the cross for the remission of sins (Romans 3:25). To fulfill this, God has set forth the propitiation of the death of Jesus and shed the sinless blood for the remission of the sins of mankind. There is no other way of remission of sins without the shedding of the blood.

Many religious leaders and philosophers always argue why not God, who so loves mankind, forgives their sins just like that? That is not the way it works. He is a *just* (righteous) God. He has to punish or penalize everyone who commits sin! If that was not the case, He would not have punished Lucifer, who was once an angel but became Satan full of evil. God punished Lucifer, who became Satan, and he is now watching over mankind as a roaring lion seeking whom he may devour (1 Peter 5:8). Cannot God punish mankind accordingly when they disobey Him? He is holy and shall be sanctified in righteousness (Isaiah 5:16).

Why Jesus Came to Defeat Satan?

Who is Jesus? What is His origin? What is the beginning of His existence? Is He someone who came into the world being born of a woman some two thousand years ago to start a new religion called Christianity? Is He like any other great personalities, like Buddha, Dalai Lama, Mohammad Nabi, Thiruvalluvar, Mahavira, Vishwamitra, Vivekananda, Mahatma Gandhi, Abraham Lincoln, and Nelson Mandela? What is the difference between them and Jesus Christ?

I have given the complete narratives of Satan in the earlier chapters. Let me give the complete narratives of Jesus Christ, which makes Him the only person who could defeat Satan. The history from birth to death about all the personalities listed above in the previous paragraph is readily available through many literary sources including the internet. I am not going to give many details about them.

1. Jesus is Alpha and Omega! That means the beginning and the end. Not like Lucifer, who was an angel before he rebelled against God and became Satan. Jesus Christ was the Word of God existing from the beginning of the entire creation. That is His kingdom. In the beginning was the Word, and the Word was with God and the Word was God (John 1:1). Maybe He was not known by the name Jesus Christ at that time.
2. Jesus was the only begotten Son of God before any other thing or matter was ever created. The term "only begotten Son" signifies the replica of God Himself (John 3:16). The only sovereign God, Jehovah, was self-existent, and Jesus was the first begotten of God. He was not a reproduction of God but begotten of God. From the human point of view in the flesh, a father can reproduce a son through a woman (mother) but not in the spiritual sense and in the spiritual realm.
3. He was present from time immemorial, and not that He just come into existence two thousand years ago being born of Virgin Mary as the world recognizes Him. That was His appearance in the human form in flesh.
4. He was present at the time of the creation of the heavens and earth and the entire universe as we see them now—the

stars, sun, moon, planets, etc. All of them were created by Him and for Him (John 1:3, Colossians 1:16).

5. He was present at the time of the recreation of the earth when it was made habitable for human existence. In the creation story as we read in the book of Genesis 1–2, God spoke the Word (Jesus), and everything came into existence. But when He created man, He said, "Let us make man in Our (plural) own image" as if He were talking to His Son, Jesus, and perhaps to the Holy Spirit too (Genesis 1:26).
6. He was with the Father when Lucifer rebelled against God and became Satan.
7. He was present when Adam and Eve were deceived and fell into sin in the Garden of Eden and God cursed mankind because of Adam and pronounced judgment against Satan and about his defeat by the seed of the woman, and Jesus knew that it was going to be Himself. He knew that He has to go to the world at God's appointed time (when the fullness of the time came) to overcome Satan and to defeat him and death too (Galatians 4:4). He was well prepared for that.
8. He knew that he should be born of a woman (Genesis 3:15) as a man in the flesh to suffer, take upon Himself the entire sin of mankind, shed His sinless blood and die on the cross, rise again from the death, defeating death also once and for all. He knew everything from the very beginning of the creation of mankind on the face of the earth.
9. He knew only through Him anyone can obtain eternal life! He is the way, the truth, and life (John 14:6).
10. He knew He will be exalted high enough to bring Satan under His feet (Philippians 2:9–10).

How Did Jesus Gain the Power to Defeat Satan?

1. He is the only begotten of God, fully divine, fully man in flesh and blood.

2. He alone could exercise the power and authority over Satan. As we saw earlier, man in his own physical strength cannot overcome and defeat the devil.
3. Man is born in sin and living in the nature of sin and has all weaknesses of the flesh.
4. Blood sacrifice is essential for the remission of sin (2 Corinthians 5:21). Sinful, corrupt, unholy blood cannot bring redemption or reconciliation as we saw earlier.
5. The demand of Satan for restitution of mankind with God for his sins could not be fulfilled with the shedding of blood through sacrifice of a lamb or a cattle or a bird.
6. Jesus Christ, when He was on the earth, although in the human form, demonstrated and proved to all, including Satan, that He is divine and has power and authority over Satan and all his power and authority and would be able to deliver mankind from the bondage of Satan (Acts 10:38).
7. He openly declared that He came to destroy all works of Satan (1 John 3:8) and gained power and authority over him, even over death which is regarded as the last enemy. He demonstrated every one of them throughout His life and in His atoning death on the cross.
8. By rising again from the death, He overcame the curse of death once and for all (1 Corinthians 15:54–56).
9. By suffering in His own body, He bought the salvation through His blood for everyone who believes in His name and atoning death and earns the reconciliation with God the Father.
10. He was exalted above every other name and everything both in heaven and on earth and things below the earth, and he became the judge over everything and the king of the life eternal (Philippians 2:9–10).

These are the things to be achieved over Satan, which Jesus alone has achieved in order to deliver anyone who believes in Him (every human being take advantage of this provision) from the bondage of Satan. Could it be possible by anyone else who appeared on

WHO RULES THE WORLD, GOD OR SATAN?

the face of the earth as great men in the above list? Or have anyone demonstrated what Jesus Christ has demonstrated both while living or in death and in resurrection? Do you think that Satan will bow to anyone? Why should he? After all, he has more power than them and has got everyone under his bondage! As long as anyone listens to him, obeys him, does everything what he tells him to do, he is not going to bother them! The very purpose for which Jesus came into this world is to destroy the works of the devil and deliver everyone under bondage of sin and sickness (1 John 3:8). He has already achieved that, and all what we have to do to be delivered is to believe in the name of Jesus and accept what He has done for us on the cross through his suffering and death and resurrection. Hallelujah!

CHAPTER 11

The Facts about the Millennium

It is also called the last dispensation for mankind before the final reconciliation and removal of curse from the earth. "In the dispensation of the fullness of times, He (the Father) might gather together in one all things in Christ, both which are in heaven and which are on earth" (Ephesians 1:10).

This millennium is called in many ways in the Scriptures.

1. One group of people who were beheaded for the witness of Christ and for the Word of God, who had not worshipped the beast, neither his image, nor received the mark upon their foreheads or in their hands lived and reigned with Christ a *thousand years* (Revelation 20:4). During this dispensational period, Satan will be bound, cast into the bottomless pit, and sealed for a thousand years. There will be *no Satan* moving around of the face of the Earth (Revelation 20:2–3).
2. It is called *the world to come*. This is the dispensation of the time between this current material world and the beginning of eternity. This millennial rule is going to take place in this very earth and the "then world therein" before the *new heaven and the new earth* is ushered in (Matthew 12:32; Ephesians 1:27, 2:7).

3. It is also called the kingdom of God on earth. Jesus has mentioned about the kingdom of God to His disciples, but none of them could understand it properly! Throughout the human history, we find kingdoms came, kingdoms fell and disappeared, but the world remains. Were all these kingdoms of God? No way! All these were satanic kingdoms. Millennium is the true kingdom of God on the face of the earth, which Jesus was often talking about with His disciples (Mark 14:25, Luke 19:11). The true King of this kingdom will be our Lord Jesus Christ, and this kingdom is going to last for one thousand years. Undisputed and unchallenged one great king! This is called the kingdom of God, but the King is going to be Jesus as promised to King David that his kingdom will be established on the earth forever. This was prophesied by Isaiah in chapter 9:6. "Unto us [world] is Son is given [Jesus] and the government shall be upon His shoulders and He is the Prince of peace." And also by Prophet Daniel: "One like the Son of Man [Jesus] came with the clouds of heaven and there was given Him dominion, glory, and a kingdom that all people, nations, and languages should serve Him" (Daniel 7:13–14). This is the Christ's millennial kingdom. This is an earthly kingdom. The capital of this kingdom will be Jerusalem, and it will be a worldwide kingdom.
4. Those who were living and missed out in the rapture will continue to live in this world as usual. There will be no presidents, prime ministers, kings, rulers of any kind. No independent powers of any kind. No more resurrection of wicked dead. They will wait for their resurrection until the day of the great and final white throne judgment. There will be governors and ambassadors sent to rule all the different nations of the world under the kingship of Jesus, from among the raptured and resurrected saints who died in Christ before the coming of the Lord, according to their deeds and witnessing for the name of Jesus Christ. They are the ones who overcame Satan by the blood of the lamb

and by the word of their testimony; they loved not their lives unto the death (Revelation 12:11). This is going to be the part of the rewards which the saints are going to receive before the final rewarding ceremony after the judgment day.

This is how the earth and the world is going to be for one thousand years. The King is Jesus. The capital is Jerusalem. The nations and languages are going to continue, ruled by the saints—that is *us*. No more Satan and presence of any evil. The length of days of living will be increased. A child will live as a child for over a hundred years. The length of life of adults will be more than hundred years, giving them an opportunity to acknowledge Jesus as their savior and repent and shun away the sins. Those who still fail to acknowledge Jesus as savior will be judged accordingly on the great white throne judgment and permanently sent to hell and later to the Lake of Fire. This is again the grace of God through Jesus Christ (Revelation 20:14).

You may think how anyone could refuse to acknowledge Jesus as their savior and Lord during that millennium. To our surprise, there are going to be many, says the Scripture! How! The sinful nature of fallen man has not changed. The Scripture says that the knowledge about Christ will fill the earth, but whether all the people will accept Him as Lord and savior? Not *all*. Satan is no more there! True! But the self-righteousness of man and the rebellious attitude do not allow them to accept Jesus. Let me remind you again. Neither Jesus is going to force them. Still their own *freewill* continue to work in them. Let us search the Scriptures.

We read about the two and final witnesses for Christ who will be revealed to the whole world and will literally demonstrate the power of God, but still the people on the earth at that time are *not* going to accept Jesus as their Lord and Savior. Instead, they will mock at the two witnesses and finally kill them by the power of Satan. All the people were watching this as spectators and never acknowledge the power of God. There is no mention about anyone getting saved at that time (Revelation chapter 11). So it looks like although the whole world will be filled with the knowledge of Jesus Christ and the glory of the Lord (Habakkuk 2:14), there seems to be not many people acknowledge Jesus as Lord and savior and no salvation taking place.

Let us read Revelation 20:7–10. When the thousand years are expired (after the millennium), Satan will be loosed out of his prison. He shall go out to deceive the nations, which are in the four quarters of the earth, and gather them together to battle against the saints. Who are these people whom Satan and his angels could gather up against the saints? They are the rebellious people still living during the millennium. People who did not acknowledge or accept Jesus to be their Lord, Savior, and King. Very unfortunate, but it is true. Again, God has to depute Michael and other angels and saints to come down and destroy Satan's entire army and take all of them to be thrown in the Lake of Fire, which is the final destination of Satan and his hosts. Anyways, the millennium is also going to come to an end. After that, the great white throne judgment is going to take place, followed by the beginning of *eternity*.

CHAPTER 12

The End of Satan and His Activities

Do you know that there is going to be a world without Satan! For many people, including Christians, this is something they are not able to comprehend. They know and believe that Satan exists, and his activities are unbelievably realistic. Most of us are thinking good and evil will exist together forever and ever. No way! God has determined the time limit for Satan's existence and activities. When that time limit is over, Satan will be removed from the earth forever. You may ask me how sure it is going to be and what is the proof or evidence for it. It is evident from scriptural, chronological, and historical and also scientific points of view. Every creation of God will have no end and may be lost forever unless God thinks otherwise or changes His mind.

It corresponds to the scientific view of the existence of the universe from time immemorial, and the life of the universe is estimated to be several billions of years. Even the scriptures do not contradict that view. Those are all nonliving things and could last forever. Only the living things have what is called a span of life, an origin and end. The life of any living thing has been found to be not more than one thousand years. Men in the early few generations have lived close to one thousand years. Even some kinds of vegetation are found to be lasting around one thousand years and not more. Scientists have found and identified trees which are close to one thousand years old but not more. According to the Scriptures and other historical evidences, man had the maximum length of 960 years of life. They all die and are removed from this earth.

The scientific claim of the universe being several billions of years old is an acceptable theory. The earth could have been existing for several millions of years, but the life on the earth has no evidence to prove that they are several billion years old. It could be easily proven that such a concept is totally impossible and utterly baseless. It is evident by the simple calculation of the human population growth. It has been proven by the same scientists, mathematicians, and computer experts that the human population is just over 7 billion as of today. If the human life has existed for several millions of years, if not billions of years as the scientists claim, how could that be possible? When you calculate the possible length of human life backward from today with the known 7 billion people, it has been proven beyond doubt that if there had been only one pair of human being (male and female) some six thousand years ago on the earth, there could be 7 billion today. Surprising! But it is true.

Let us look in the authenticated statistics about the growth of human population.

- The first billion was reached in 1800 (after Noah's flood).
- The second billion was reached in 1927 (127 years later).
- The third billion was reached in 1960 (33 years later).
- The fourth billion was reached in 1974 (14 years later).
- The fifth billion was reached in 1987 (13 years later).
- The sixth billion was reached in 1999 (12 years later).
- The seventh billion was reached in 2011 (12 years later).
- The population is expected to reach 10 billion in 2050 (estimated).

It took only 210 years for the population to reach 7 billion from 1 billion in AD 1800. It could be possible for the population to reach 1 billion from just one pair of human beings (one male and one female) some 5,800 years since Adam and Eve were created. Taking into consideration the length of life of individuals and the great many natural disasters and destructions caused by men and also divine interventions as in the times of Noah's flood, the scientists and mathematicians also agree to these figures because they determined this population growth is possible only over the period of six thousand years and could not be more. They are also projecting the human population to reach 10 billion by 2050. At this rate of population growth, if there was one pair of humans, say 1 million years ago (or even one hundred thousand years ago), what would have been the population of humans today? Do we find them on the face of the earth? Where are they? The truth remains that the present-day population of humans is little over 7 billion *only*. How could the same scientists and mathematicians still claim that human life was in existence since millions of years ago? Let us be honest about it! This disproves the evolution theory straight away! Creation is the *only* possibility.

The History of Mankind Will Last Only 7,000 Years

Mankind is not going to live in this world (on the earth) forever. The history of mankind is going to come to an end. It started approximately six thousand years ago and will come to end at the end of seven thousand years. That is at the end of 3000 years AD. We have already passed 2017 years. That is to say that man has lived on the face of this earth for nearly 6017 years already. When you think of it, it may surprise many, including the scientists, statisticians, and mathematicians. But it is the fact of the matter. God is Alpha and Omega. Everlasting (Genesis 21:33). "I AM THAT I AM" Exodus 3:14. Jesus is Alpha and Omega (Revelation 1:8), and neither Satan nor human is Alpha and Omega. They had a beginning, and they are going to have an end.

We cannot calculate or stipulate the time of the origin of Satan. The Scriptures tells us that Satan was not created as Satan. When the angels and other heavenly beings were created, an angel by the name Lucifer was also crated besides Michael and Gabriel. These three angels are otherwise called archangels. Lucifer was also called the Morning Star. There was no Satan at that time. There was heaven; all the created beings were there. Michael and Gabriel were kept in the heaven. Lucifer was kept on the earth to take care of the pre-Adamite earth. Each of them had different authorities, powers, functions, and responsibilities. Michael was the chief archangel and the head of the hosts of God. Gabriel was the messenger angel to bring messages from God to the occupants of the earth. Lucifer was head of the hosts of those angels who are created to worship the only sovereign God all the time (24/7, or round the clock). Each of these archangels were given one-third of the total number of angels to serve God under their leadership. Michael and Gabriel were kept in heaven, but Lucifer was kept on the earth to rule the inhabitants of the earth. He was also commanded to present himself with a report of what he was doing on the earth at a time appointed by God. This is what we read and understand in the book of Job chapters 1–2.

Rebellion of Lucifer and How He Became Satan

Regarding the time when the rebellion took place, we have no idea, but it is a fact that Satan was present in the Garden of Eden when God created Adam and put them in the Garden of Eden. How long since he rebelled and was cursed to be Satan? We have no idea. The story of the present human race begins from the creation of Adam and Eve in the Garden of Eden. But the complete record of how Lucifer rebelled and became Satan is very clearly given in the Scriptures. Let us consider the story of Satan's rebellion and the beginning of the curse.

Many people argue how could anyone rebel against an all-powerful God? True! A very good and reasonable question. As long as anyone is in the presence of God all the time, he is not going to rebel against God. Moreover, in the presence of God, no freewill is given to anyone to operate themselves. But unfortunately, Lucifer was not in the presence of God all times, and he was given freewill to operate and function on his own and rule the earth. This is very evident from the passages we are going to consider below from the Scriptures.

Isaiah 14:12–15 says, "How art thou fallen from heaven, O Lucifer, here is where we get his original name, son of the morning, how art thou cut down to the ground, which did weaken the nations.

For thou has said in thine heart; I will ascend into heaven [which tells us that he was *not* in the heavens] and I will exalt my throne above the stars of God; I will sit also upon the mount of the congregation in the sides of the North [that was where the Garden of Eden, the Garden of God was situated]. Yet thou shalt be brought down to hell, to the sides of the pit."

This tells us the following:

- Lucifer was *not* in heaven all the time. He was visiting heaven at God's appointed time (Job chapter 1 and 2).
- When he says "I will ascend into heaven," it is obvious that he was below the heavens and very precisely on the earth.
- He knows that the throne of God is in heaven.
- He also knows that he cannot build his throne where God's throne is, so he said to himself that he will build his throne among the stars.

Let us read the other passage: "Thou [Lucifer] has been in Eden, the Garden of God ... Thou art the anointed cherub [on par with archangel], that covered, I [God] has set thee so, thou art upon the Holy mountain of God, thou was perfect in thy ways from the day you were created until iniquity [rebellion] was found in thee" (Ezekiel 28:13–15). It clearly tell us that it was his rebellion that brought him down as a cursed being on to the earth.

We don't have to argue and debate whether this account about Satan is true or correct or whatever. The fact remains that the whole world today is *evil*, and based on the current factual situation, something had happened earlier, and this is the best account available to say that from some time earlier, Satan, the total embodiment of evil, came into existence, and that cannot be denied by anyone. The fact also remains that God did not create him as Satan, but he became *evil* and calls himself Satan! Or we call him Satan. So the date of origin of Satan cannot be assessed because the time of occurrence of that rebellion is not given in the Scriptures. But the date when man was created could be assessed. And the end of mankind on the face of the earth is also predetermined. What is going to happen after also are clearly explained and foretold. That is why it is important to understand the population criteria.

Everything Which Was Created after the First Rebellion Has to Come to an End

Things which do not have an origin but came in to existence by creation in due course are going to have an end. Only those who are self-existent can go on forever and ever without end. For example, the Father, the Son, and the Holy Spirit. The universe is God's creation and is subject to change, alter, or could be annihilated. God the Father is the sovereign self-existent entity. Jesus is the only begotten Son of God. The word beget has vast meaning, and it is not just producing a child in the natural sense, like someone becomes a father when he produces a child. The Father, also known or called as Jehovah (Elohim, Adonai), did not become Father because he produced any child. He is called or addressed as the Father because He is the source of all living beings and things. When He created Adam, breathed in his nostrils, he became a living soul. The Father did not get his name as Father because He created Adam. In the practical sense, Adam was His first earthly son as we read in Luke 3:38 where Adam was designated as Son of God although He was a created being.

Only Jesus Christ was designated as His only begotten Son; it has a totally different meaning. He is the exact replica of the Father in every nature and character of God. He could manifest and exhibit the same characters, power, and all authority as if the Father was present there. He should not be classified or addressed as a lesser god or lower than the Father, less powerful, etc. This can be clearly understood from John 1:1–3. In the beginning was the Word, and the Word was with God, and the Word was God. All things were made by Him, and without Him nothing was made that was made.

As we have seen earlier, mankind has passed 6016 years according to English and Jewish calendars. Mankind is waiting for the millennial rule by Jesus Christ to begin or start. That will last for another ten thousand years. It could start to happen anytime now. First, the rapture of the true church, followed by the tribulation for seven years, including the revelation of the antichrist. During this time, Jerusalem will be taken over by the antichrist. Then Jesus Christ will appear openly with the sound of a trumpet, and the battle of Armageddon will take place. I am not going into the full details of the war, which is very hard to follow. The war is going to happen in the northeast of Jerusalem and a very vast desert. The war will last just for a day. The Antichrist will be killed. The antichrist is not Satan himself. Satan will be taken into captivity and will be locked in the bottomless pit for one thousand years, along with all the evil spirits. There will be destruction of one-third of the (world) population of mankind. The rest of the people continue to live in this world, and Jesus Christ Himself will be the only ruler and king, and the whole world will be under His righteous rule for one thousand years. Satan along with all fallen angels, evil spirits, and all that belong to him will not be there on the earth because all of them will be locked under the earth in the *bottomless pit* for one thousand years.

Many are wondering what it means by bottomless pit. A pit should have a bottom. Then only it could be called as a pit. Quite true. To understand this clearly, we have to find out where the pit opens and where it ends. The Bible mentions many times the phrase called "beneath the earth." Even Jesus knew about it and understood the *deep* or the bottom less pit when demonic spirits pleaded to Him not to send them to the deep (Luke 8:31). All these tell us that the bottomless pit, Hades and the Hell itself, which is also called the Lake of Fire, are right under our feet in the middle portion of the earth. The center (middle portion) of the earth holds the hottest stratum, which could otherwise be called the Lake of Fire, the final destiny of the satanic realm. The temperature of that hottest portion is estimated to be six thousand degree Celsius. When this hottest stratum of the earth burst open through the mountains, we see them and call them as volcanoes. The temperatures of these volcanic eruptions by the time they reach the surface of the earth are estimated to be three thousand degree Celsius. The Bible describes that the hell has enlarged herself and opened her mouth without measure, and multitude of people shall descend into it (Isaiah 5:14). This is what Jesus meant when He said to those on His left-hand side on the day of the great white throne judgment that "depart from me, you cursed, in to everlasting fire, prepared for the devils and his angels since the beginning of this world" (Matthew 25:41–46). One such opening was seen recently by a naval admiral when he flew in his plane over the North Pole. As he was approaching the North Pole, his plane compass failed to work. He could feel very hot air blowing over his plane raising the outside temperature of the plane, and somehow he forced himself away from that hot zone in the polar region and returned back safely. He describes it as a mouth of a big hole as wide as a mile's length, and it looks like the mouth of a funnel sucking everything when they are in a close range. This could be the mouth of the bottomless pit.

We all know that the earth is a sphere. It is a globe. If you travel across the globe, you will exit on the other side of the globe. But you cannot pass through the middle hottest portion of the earth. The pit could possibly have many openings like this from many sides of the earth like what the naval admiral saw in the North Pole. Even if there is more than one mouth like this to the pit, obviously, it does not have a bottom. All the mouth-like opening works like the mouth of a funnel and meet at the center, which is the hottest portion under the earth. So these pits do not have a bottom. That is why the Scriptures always mention that as the bottomless pit. Satan and all the demonic spirits will be sent to the bottomless pit, tied, locked, and sealed for one thousand years during the millennial rule of our Lord Jesus Christ.

CHAPTER 13

The Final Judgment of Mankind and Satan

The entire mankind is going to be judged. For many, it may be incomprehensible or even unacceptable. This is because we look at the whole picture of the world and mankind from our (human) point of view or perspective. We fail to look at it from God's point of view and perspective. It is going to be hard to understand. Religious scholars and theologians refuse to accept this doctrine or theology based on one fundamental thinking. God is *love and full of grace*, and He will not punish or destroy the best of His creation, mankind. They don't want to understand that He is *full of love and grace*, but at the same time, He is *holy and righteous*. If love and grace is one side of the coin, holiness and righteousness is the other side. Throughout the Scriptures and the history of mankind, God has revealed it in many ways, by many of His actions and judgments. He never compromises with unrighteousness and injustice. In all occasions, He has kept His justice and protected His righteousness

We can see and observe it in the very Garden of Eden. When He created everything, He saw them to be *good*. Finally, when He created man and the woman, He saw and found them to be *very good*. Nobody wants to think of the feelings and the hurt He would have felt when Adam and Eve were deceived, disobeyed His commandments, and fell short of the glory with which He had clothed them. Many of us think that God does not have feelings; rather, he should not have. I could feel it. It broke His heart into million pieces. The best of His creations, with whom He could communicate and share the joy of heavens, dissolved like vapor into the air. The other side is the mockery from Satan. You brought man in my place, and see now how I have brought him under my slavery. God's justice stood above all. He punished Satan when he rebelled against Him; now He can't let go man for what he has done.

He did not change His mind or alter the plan. From human point of view, we could lay down a number of options. Do you want me to list them? Because we are very intelligent people and could offer at least four to five options. But God does not change. He had to provide *only one* option, which will restore and reconcile mankind back to Him and destroy the works of the devil once and for all by one act. That is why he has to send Jesus in the fullness of times to accomplish both together. Because he decided the strategy on the very same day of Adam's fall, He announced it right there in the Garden of Eden in front of Satan. The very same moment He decided the destiny of Satan as well (Genesis 3:1–15). You don't have to be a great scholar to understand this. This is very straightforward and revealed for us to understand. Don't complicate it and get confused. From God's perspective, He has kept his justice and made the provisions for mankind because He loved them dearly. Satan thought he had won, but truly, he was *cut to his size*. God is always the *victor*.

The greatest loss to man is the loss of communication with God. He was left alone and all by himself. No one to counsel him, guide him, help him, and nobody around him to share anything. The only guy available close to him is Satan. Until he fell, God was coming to visit him every day. But now he has to call on God for everything. The only one available to his beg and call is devils and satanic spirits. Awful it is indeed! There started the calamity and the disaster. Like Satan and his angels were cursed when they rebelled against God, Adam and Eve were cursed to suffer until the redemption comes. Dear people, don't blame and curse God at any time in any circumstances and for any of your sufferings. God is not the reason, and He is not the source of any of our sufferings.

God let go everything because He is *just* and made *all necessary provisions* for mankind because He is full of *love and grace*. It may be hard for you to understand in the beginning, but when you experience and taste His love, it will be unparalleled. Many of us don't want to do it, because our hearts are so hardened with unbelief.

Noah's Flood: An Act of Love or Holiness?

For many, it is a good biblical story to tell the Sunday school children. For them, the Ark will be best attraction. Once they understand the story, they will never forget it for the rest of their lives. Very good! But what is the lesson we are able to get to their mind. Nothing. Why did God do it? What made Him get so mad on people and decide to destroy them in total and save only Noah and his family? This is what the Scripture reads: "God saw that the wickedness of man was great in the earth and that every imagination of the thoughts of his heart was only evil continually" (Genesis 6:5). "It grieved Him at his heart" (Verse 6). He decided to destroy the man I have created, the beasts and the creeping things and the fowls of the air in total. Why? Does that mean His love has gone and disappeared? No! His holiness prevailed over His love. He is holy that He cannot stand sin. Sin is the fruit of Satan. Satan knew pretty well that God will not tolerate sin, and He will take action. For Satan, God executing judgment on mankind and destroy them is a pleasure. He would love it because all of them are going to end up with him in Hades. It grieved God's heart, and He regretted for having created man on the earth. All these spirits were under bondage with Satan. After Jesus died on the cross and was buried, He went to these spirits and gave them the good news of salvation through His death on the cross. And many accepted His offer and believed in Jesus and was taken with Him into paradise. What a glorious provision because of Jesus!

Destruction of Sodom and Gomorrah was another example of holiness prevailing over love! Of course, God loves mankind and wants them to live a fearless, happy life in this world and is given enough time and opportunity to accept the love offer given to them through Jesus. "God so loved the world that He gave His only begotten Son Jesus, that whosoever believes in Him should not perish, but have everlasting life" (John 3:16). If we reject this offer, we have no rights to claim salvation when God executes judgment.

The Exodus: An Act of Grace or Righteousness

His holiness and righteousness were revealed and established when He delivered the Israelites from under the bondage of Egyptians. The story needs not be repeated because the whole world knew, and the history has been clearly documented. I am not going into the details of why such a bondage was permitted by God and why a man like Moses was chosen and sent to deliver them. That is entirely God's sovereignty, and I am not going into that character of God to explain. Well, Moses was sent; the Exodus began. In the process of deliverance, God had to bring upon Egypt ten different plagues to ease the heart of Pharaoh. To many people who do not have the knowledge of the background, this looks like God has mercilessly punished the Egyptians in order to liberate the Israelites. It is not so. Again, God executed justice and established righteousness. I know it is hard to comprehend, but from God's perspective, that is what is right!

Now, according to historical records, six hundred thousand men with women and children left Egypt. According to the mathematicians, it could easily be 2 million people. They were taken through the longest route to reach Canaan, the Promised Land. Why? Again, God's righteousness has to be established. His holiness also has to be proven and has to be understood by the people of Israel. Sin was expressly demonstrated by them. He gave them Ten Commandments. They disobeyed some and violated many. Altogether, they sinned against God and kindled His anger. All of them has to be punished, and justice has to be established. Only two persons, namely Caleb and Joshua, were found to be in perfect obedience to God. Even Moses himself failed. Now God's character of holiness and righteousness had to be proven and established in line with the judgment He executed on the people of Egypt. He cannot be partial. He punished and destroyed 2 million Israelites in the wilderness after they have been delivered from Egypt. Now let us be honest! Is God holy and righteous? Does that mean that He was not loving and merciless? No way! This is the hardest part of God's character to understand. God is sandwiched between love and holiness, between grace and righteousness. Which will prevail? His holiness and righteousness. From the human world view, this is very hard to accept. For them, God should only full of *love and grace*. Think for yourself!

Grace versus Righteousness

We have learned that holiness and righteousness is God's inherent characters. God will never compromise on those things. He has shown it, demonstrated it, and proven it beyond any doubt. The scriptures give us an indication that that was a period of four hundred years of silence from God until Jesus was born on the earth. Many prophecies were given to men about His coming, but there was a silence. Mankind was totally in the dark about the knowledge of God. The law was in operation, but nobody cared about it. Peace and justice are totally forgotten entities. Many different religions have appeared to seek and know God but not much of a significance. In short, the world was in total confusion. Religious rituals proliferated all over the world. The only section of the people who had some knowledge about the true living God is the Judaic community. They were expecting the Messiah to come, but when Jesus came, they disregarded Him (John 1:11). Moses came and brought the Law. Jesus came with full of grace and truth (John 1:17). Why is grace so important?

God is holy and righteous. He can neither tolerate nor compromise with sin. So how can a man in sin be justified without judgment? According to the Scriptures (Psalms 14:2, 53:2; Romans 3:23), all men have sinned and come short of the glory of God. There is none righteous. No, not one! There is none who seeks after God. So the judgment is reserved for everyone who is ever born on the earth, beginning from Adam. Whether anyone was righteous or not has to be judged by a righteous person (Jesus, because *no man* is righteous according to the standard of God). God has designated Him already to judge the entire world without any prejudice. He was sinless, ever righteous, and will be righteous forever.

But the same Jesus was sent into this world two thousand years ago, and He is full of grace and truth to save all those who are lost in sin. His appearance as Messiah on the earth is withholding God's righteousness not to be revealed from time to time. The law is held obsolete because of the revelation of grace through Jesus Christ. Jesus completed all the demands of the law and finished all the works He was sent for, including destroying the works of the devil. I have been observing many preachers ignoring Satan and his activities in their preaching and teachings, which has let him to be more active than ever before. Grace is available for all those who seek after it. For them who believe on the Lord Jesus Christ for their remission of sins, they will be made righteous to meet with God's standard of righteousness. Not just by talking about, promising about it or by any other means. It is every individual's responsibility to accept that the only way is Jesus to be made righteous and reconcile with God. There are too many false interpretations floating in the Christian circle about grace; beware of them! Of course, justification in definitely not by works but by grace only in God's way and in our own way! Remember, *grace* is unmerited favor from God received as a gift freely by faith in Jesus Christ.

So it is mandatory that *all men* will be subjected to God's final judgment. "It is appointed unto men once to die and after this the judgment" (Hebrews 9:27). He created man. He gave them the law to follow, obey, and keep. He did not care about it. Then He made an alternative redemption provision by grace through Jesus Christ. Mankind rejected that also. Because of grace, the judgment is only withheld and not canceled. For all those who accepted this great and valuable provision of salvation by grace through faith in Jesus, there are some exceptions. All those who are justified by faith and were taken away at the time of rapture, when Jesus returns to take away the saints, are the most privileged ones who will not face the final judgment. All the others will face the white throne judgment (Revelation 20:11).

When the one thousand years of millennial rule of Jesus Christ is over, which concludes the history of mankind on the face of the earth, Satan and his angels are going to be released for some time (which is not prescribed in the Scriptures). He is going to be punished forever.

"When the thousand years are expired, Satan shall be loosed out of prison and he goes out to deceive nations from all quarters of the earth, to gather them to gather them together to battle; the number of whom is as the sand of the sea, and compassed the camp of the saints about and the city of Jerusalem, and gathers them to battle against them. But the fire came from heaven over them and devoured them" (Revelation 20:7–9). Then the devil that deceived them was captured and cast into the lake of fire and brimstone, where the beast and false prophet are already and shall be tormented forever and ever (Revelation 20:10). Then the death and hell were also cast in to the fire. This is the *second death*. And whosoever was not found written in the Book of Life was cast in to the lake of fire (Revelation 20:10–15). That is the end of Satan forever.

The Final White Throne Judgment

This marks the end of mankind on the face of the earth and also the end of Satan and all evil and curse from the face of the earth forever and ever. Many argue that earth will not be totally removed or annihilated. It will pass from one stage to another and will be either recreated or replenished in to something new. The scripture does not endorse this view.

Let us look in to the Scriptures as it is described in Revelation 20:11–15. John sees a GREAT WHITE THRONE and someone seated on it. It could not be anybody else other than Jesus Christ because He is the one assigned to do that job by the Father the moment He rose again from the dead and ascended up to be seated on the right hand of God. Where the great white throne is kept, placed? I don't know! The moment He (Jesus) sat on this white throne, the old heaven and the old earth fled away (meaning disappeared) because it also confirms that there was *no place* found for them. I do not want to raise a question to analyze or debate on how it will be possible. My simple and humble answer would be, it is not my problem, and it is God's problem. The Scriptures says so and I believe it. (Revelation 20:11)

At this time we have to compare what Jesus Himself said about this White throne judgment. These are His own saying. When the Son of Man (Jesus Christ Himself) shall come in His glory and all His holy angels with Him, then He shall sit on the *throne* of His glory (Matthew 25:31–46). (Again, many are curious to debate on this and want to bring lot more confusion.) The whole passage very clearly narrates the picture of the judgment of the righteous and the wicked. Let us *not* worry about *how* and *why* and *where*—that is not ours to understand—but let us get ready to face the judgment seat of Christ. The Scripture says *all* nations, both wicked and righteous. In Revelation, we see *all* the *dead*. It only tells us that there are going to be people from two sources. According to the Scriptures, *all mankind* have to face judgment. All the dead before the day of judgment will be raised up and gathered up before the great white throne. At the same time, all the living through the millennium will also be brought together before the great white throne. Everyone was judged according to his works—whether righteous or wicked, how he was made righteous either by believing in Christ or considered wicked because he rejected Christ. I like the way the proceedings went through.

Jesus Christ need not do anything. He just shows His right hand, and all the righteous go to that side. He just show His left hand, and all the wicked go to that side. Of course, the same thing is pictured in a slightly different way. Before Jesus, who is now seated on the throne, the Book of Life was opened. Automatically, everyone whose names were in the Book of Life walked over to the right-hand side. All those whose names were not found in the Book of Life automatically walked to the left. What a remarkable judgment. Then Jesus to those who are on the *right*, He says, "Come ye blessed of my Father. Go and inherit the kingdom prepared for you." They will enter the eternal life. And to all those who stand on the *left*, He says, "*Depart* from me, ye cursed into everlasting *fire* prepared for the devil and his angels," and they end up in everlasting punishment (Revelation 20:14). *Death and hell* will be cast into the Lake of Fire. This is the *second death*.

CHAPTER 14

The Second Death: The Final Destiny of Satan

God is holy and righteous (just). This is His inherent character. God cannot compromise in these characters. He can never be unholy or unrighteous. If you really want to weigh the importance between holiness and love, holiness weigh supreme. If you want to weigh the importance between righteousness and grace, righteousness weighs supreme. Here lies the problem. God is both holy and righteous and also full of love and grace. Don't get me wrong; I am not saying God is not loving and graceful at all. He is full of truth and mercy.

But the inherent character of Satan is just the opposite. He is the total embodiment of unholy and unrighteousness. He is full of hatred, enmity, ungraceful, unlawful, merciless, and full of evil. Bible describes him as Father of lies. There is no truth in him whatsoever. He has blinded the eyes of all people, including the so-called Christians and the Christian churches.

From the very beginning, he proved to be a liar when he deceived Adam and Eve in the Garden of Eden. He is tirelessly carrying on this job till today, and is he going to continue the same into all eternity? If so, if God is going to allow it into eternity, what is the purpose? Is he at some point of time going to be given a chance to repent and become a goody-goody guy? Impossible it is, indeed! Because some of the false teachings stand on the belief that after death all the souls will go to a place called purgatory (as the Catholics say and believe) and there all the evil souls will get another opportunity to be saved, and finally all the souls will reach heaven only! The Bible does not endorse this view at all!

God's character of being full of love and grace does not mean anyone could be ungodly and still God has to love him! No, sir! The Bible does guarantee that at all. Don't be mistaken and be carried away by such teachings. Throughout the Scriptures, we find whenever the people behaved ungodly, He brought judgment upon them! The Lord of Hosts shall be exalted in judgment, and God that is holy shall be sanctified in righteousness (Isaiah 5:16). This is His genuine character. He neither compromised with His Holiness nor with His righteousness at any time, at any cost. Who are we to judge God and His character?

What Does the Bible Actually Mean by Second Death?

First of all, the Bible talks about the second death only in the Book of Revelation. Throughout the Bible, death is vividly discussed. Death entered into the world only after Adam and Eve fell into sin. Death never existed before. When Adam and Eve sinned, they were literally separated from God. We call as the spiritual death for our understanding because we have to give some name to that. Death in its true sense means separation. To differentiate the spiritual death from the bodily death, we have given it another name as physical death. That is why the meaning of the second death is confusing. Moreover, there is no reference of second death in the Bible except in the book of Revelation. In the physical death, we all know that the soul and spirit get separated from the body, and that person is declared to be dead. The soul together with the spirit, which is dwelling in the physical body made of flesh and blood, leaves the body and takes up an immortal status. How long this status of the soul and spirit is in this immortal state, we have to study and learn in the light of the Scriptures.

The Bible also talks about spiritual death. There seems to be a lot of confusion about this. Some say all men are spiritually dead already because we are in a state of separation from God because of our sins (Isaiah 59:1). This is totally understandable and acceptable because all have sinned and come short of the glory of God (Romans 3:26), which clearly indicates that we are separated from God in every sense. No man is able to see God as long he is in the sinful state because spiritual death has already preceded the physical death. This is understandable and agreed upon by almost everyone. The Bible also declares that *no man* has seen God at any time. The spiritual death has occurred first in everyone's life, and he continues to be in that state until he gets saved. So when the Bible talks about "It is appointed unto men once to die and then judgment," it clearly indicates the physical death everyone has to go through (Hebrews 9:27). So the other school of thought that the *second death* is spiritual death, meaning a total separation from God throughout all eternity, makes no sense. We are all spiritually dead already, and we are restored back to "spiritually alive" status reconciled with God through the washing away of our sins by the blood of Jesus through grace by faith. So these people are not going to face a *second death*. Now the question is, who are those people who will face second death, and why?

To understand the meaning of the second death, we must allow the Bible to speak for itself. First of all, the Bible never talks about the second death until the last book of the Bible. So this is something which need not be thrown into any kind of debate because it is going to happen after our physical death. It gives us an indication how to escape this second death. The truth we have to know now is our spiritually dead state and how to be saved to regain our lost state.

The teaching of the second death throws a lot of light on the judgment, which is going to come on the *ungodly*. I prefer to use the word *ungodly* because all those who are ungodly are going to be thrown in the Lake of Fire, which is the second death. We need not list all those who are going to receive this punishment. Everyone who does not live according to the ordinances of God are classified as ungodly, and all ungodly will face this punishment of getting thrown into the Lake of Fire, which is the second death. Remember, this is the result of Jesus's final white throne judgment.

Who will escape this punishment? And on whom the second death has no power or jurisdiction is described in the Bible. Let us look into it. The following are the ones who will escape the second death (total extinction):

1. "He that overcomes [overcomers] shall not be hurt of the second death" (Revelation 2:11).
2. "Blessed and holy is he that hath part in the first resurrection, on such the second death has no power" (Revelation 20:6).
3. "Whosoever was not found written in the book of life was cast in to the Lake of Fire—second death" (Revelation 20:14–15).
4. All the ungodly [fearful, unbelieving, abominable, murderers, whoremongers, sorcerers, idolaters, all liars] shall have their part in the second death (Revelation 21:8).

All the ungodly people are distinguished from the godly people. Godly people are those who are overcomers, partakers of the first resurrection (including those who are transformed into spiritual bodies), whose names are found written in the Book of Life.

What Is the First Resurrection and Why the Second Death Has No Power over Them?

For the Lord (Jesus) Himself shall descend from heaven with a shout (a call of preparation for action) with the voice of the archangel, and with the trump of God (this one is the trump of God and not the trumpet of the seventh angel found in Revelation 11:15), and the dead in Christ shall rise first. This is the first resurrection. Praise God! These are all those who died in Christ, and quite surely the second death is not going to have any power over them.

To understand the trump of God, let us compare what happened at the tomb of Lazarus of Bethany, the brother of Mary and Martha (John 11:43–44). Jesus, at the tomb of Lazarus, cried with a loud voice (like a trump), and he that was dead came forth to life.

But this is not the first resurrection for Lazarus. This is only to prove that Jesus Christ is the resurrection and life. He has to later die the physical death after which to face the judgment seat of Jesus. In the case of the first resurrection, it is going to be the archangel who is going to call all the dead in Christ to rise because Jesus is coming to receive all those who are His.

These are definitely privileged people, but not the most privileged people. The *most* privileged people are the ones who will be caught up (rapture, transformed into spiritual bodies, not tasting the physical death whatsoever) together with them in the clouds to meet the Lord in the midair, and so shall we ever be with the Lord (1 Thessalonians 4:16–17). That is why these people are called the *blessed and holy* people, and the second death will have no power over them. They will be with the Lord ruling the earth throughout the millennium and will be present at the time of the final judgment. What a glorious privilege for the ones who live and die in Christ! Finally, all those who have died in Christ and all those who will be caught up transformed into the spiritual body. They will neither taste the physical death nor have any part in the *second death*. What a glorious blessing and privilege! Praise God!

Let us consider the following texts and contexts in the Bible:

- "For a little while [short and limited time, not eternally] and wicked [ungodly] *shall not be*, yea, thou shall diligently consider his place [hell] and it shall not be" (Psalm 37:10).
- "But the wicked shall perish, and the enemies of the Lord shall be as the fat of the lambs: they shall consume: into smoke they will consume away" (Psalm 37:20).
- "I have seen the wicked in great power, and spreading himself like a green bay tree. Yet he shall *pass away*, and lo, he was *not* yea I sought him, but he could *not be found*" (Psalm 37:35–36).

Although the psalmist said then that wicked shall not be anymore, we still find them living and continue to do wickedness even now. When are they going to end or pass away? Surely, they will be destroyed after the final day of judgment? And then they are gone forever, and you can neither see them nor find the place they were.

"Let the sinners be consumed out of the earth, and the wicked shall be *no more*" (Psalm 104:35). Psalmist says let the wicked be *consumed* out of the earth. He was a Prophet and with his prophetic knowledge he felt at some point of time the wicked will be totally destroyed or consumed and they shall not be any more anywhere to be found.

"*Consume them* [wicked] in wrath; consume them that they may not be" (Psalm 59:13). King David, the psalmist, was very much aware of the wrath of God. How furious it is going to be. God character is described as a consuming fire (Hebrews 12:29). David was man of zeal for God, and He could not stand the wicked behaving against God.

"The Lord *preserves* all them that love Him: but all the wicked He will *destroy*" (Psalm 145:20). Here we read God will preserve them whom He *loves*. He will destroy all the wicked. The word *destroy* here is used against God's preservation. *To preserve* means to keep, to protect, to nourish and cherish, and this could go on forever and ever in to all eternity. To *destroy* means to bring an end to it, extinguish it, or annihilate it. This process need not take into all eternity. The most severe punishment will be there before their total destruction, and thereafter, they are no more.

"[O Lord,] Your hand shall find out all your enemies: thy right hand shall find out those that hate Thee [ungodly]. Thou shall make them as fiery oven in the time of your *anger*: the Lord will swallow them up in His wrath, and the fire shall devour [swallow] them" (Psalm 21:8–9).

Just think of God, who has been merciful and patient for over seven thousand years to mankind in the earth bearing their wickedness. He gave them His own begotten Son as a sacrifice for their own salvation. He sent them a number of witnesses and evangelists to preach to them the gospel. Despite all God's provisions to repent and come back to Him, the ungodly rejected Jesus and hated God, and hence, His wrath is kindled against them. Remember God is a just God. Mark the words that He will swallow and devour them.

"And the destruction of the transgressors and of the sinners shall be together, and they that forsake the Lord shall be *consumed*" (Isaiah 1:28). It simply means that they shall be consumed and could never be found again.

"For, behold the day cometh, that shall burn as an oven; and all the proud [Satan and his battalion], yea, and all that do wickedly [ungodly], shall be as stubble; and the day cometh that shall burn them up, said the Lord of Hosts, that it shall leave them neither root nor branch" (Malachi 4:1). This very clearly indicates that all the ungodly shall be burnt up without any trace of them left behind. Neither root nor a branch shall be left behind. They all will become nonexistent.

"The last enemy that shall be destroyed [abolished] is death" (1 Corinthians 15:26). In Revelation, John specifically mentions in chapter 20:14 the *death and hell* were cast into the Lake of Fire. Paul indicates that the final enemy, the *death*, will be destroyed or abolished when he talks about the immortality and eternal life in heaven with the Lord Jesus Christ. He does not visualize death, and hell is going to be eternal.

The following definitions are taken from *The American Heritage Dictionary of the English Language*:

Destroy:

(a) To ruin completely; spoil so that restoration is not possible; consume.
(b) To tear down or break up; raze; demolish.
(c) To do away with; get rid of; put an end to.
(d) To kill; to extinguish.

Perish:

(a) To die, especially in a violent manner.
(b) To pass from existence; disappear gradually.

Consume:

- (a) To destroy as by fire.
- (b) To use up waste (time, energy, money etc.).
- (c) To waste away; perish.

The following are from *Collins Dictionary*:

Destroy: Does not exist anymore.
Perish: If people perish, they die as a result of very harsh conditions.
Consume: To eat up fuel, energy, or time, leaving no traces behind.
Abolish: To put an end to. To stop.
Dissolve: A matter gets dissolved until it disappears.

When we view the context in which these phrases are used connected to the Lake of Fire, it very well means it is going to disappear and not going to exist anymore.

CHAPTER 15

Eternal Life versus Eternal Punishment

What Is Eternal Life?

Every believer has some idea about eternal life. Over all, they know it is the life after our physical death. True, we need not have any doubt that. But if we are sure about the eternal life, we must try to understand where we are going to spend it and with whom. Many will say simply in heaven, of course! Do you know where heaven is? Ah! I am not sure! Do you know at least with whom? I am happy to hear the answer with Jesus by many of them. Praise God! I thing we must have the complete knowledge and understanding about eternal life.

1. Eternal life is a gift of God to those who are saved (John 3:15–16, Romans 6:23, 1 John 5:11). It is promised for every believer now and will be given as gift after the judgment.
2. The souls and the spirits of the righteous (saints) which have reached the immortal state after the physical death are *resting* and being *comforted* in a place called *paradise*—Jesus also referred to it in the parable of the rich man and the poor Lazarus (Luke 16:23–31)—and will receive the reward of eternal life after the final day of judgment (Matthew 25:46).

3. That eternal life will have no end and is everlasting.
4. The enjoyment and activities during the eternal life will vary depending upon God's will, plan, and purpose. The privilege to enjoy eternal life depends on rewards for our own activities while we were on earth.
5. Eternal life starts only after the day of judgment and not immediately after death. The soul and the spirit gets into the state of immortality and is waiting for the final judgment.

What Is Eternal Punishment?

Is that phrase properly translated from the original context, and what does the Scriptures mean by that?

1. Punishment need not be eternal. Why should it be eternal, and what is the purpose?
2. Punishment is normally of two kinds. Corporal punishment and capital punishment. Corporal punishment is usually mild chastisement with an intention to correct or to give another chance to repent and change the course of life of any convicted person. Capital punishment is legal killing of a convicted person as to end his life or extinguish him. No more chance to repent or whatever. The phrase *eternal punishment* in the Scriptures means capital punishment. I am not trying to be judgmental but trying to rationalize hell's eternity.
3. The ungodly (unrighteous, wicked, and evil) were kept under suffering of some kind for all their deeds during their earthly life and are reserved for final judgment in a place called Hades (the place they are kept awaiting final judgment). In the parable of the rich man and the poor Lazarus in Luke 16:23–31, we are able to understand many facts about torment in Hades and later in hell.
    a. The rich man who is now resting in Hades (abyss or whatever you want to call it) feels the torment

by flames (not the real hell fire) and realizes his folly during his life on earth.
b. He regrets over the deeds he has committed.
c. He feels absolute hopelessness to escape from this misery.
d. He clearly understands the eternal separation from God and loss forever.
e. His name was neither given nor mentioned by Jesus Christ, which means his name has been removed (blotted out) from the Book of Life, and he is going to be thrown into the Lake of Fire, which is the second death, and he shall be remembered no more.

4. Satan and his associates will be going through the same kind of suffering and torment in the bottomless pit, also referred to as Hades, during the one thousand years of bondage. Even now, they are in some kind of distress, agony, and suffering, and that is why they are so jealous of human beings and want to give them torment and torture. We are victims of that vengeance of Satan as long as we live in this world (1 Peter 5:8).
5. The Bible clearly indicates that Satan, his angels, and all those who are associated with him also will have to face the final judgment and will be thrown into hell, and then death and hell together will be thrown into the Lake of Fire and extinguished. Hell is not the Lake of Fire. There will be no more death after that forever. Since there is no more death, there is no need for Hades and hell anymore.
6. Eternal punishment is equal to capital punishment, and there's no more second chance to repent and come back to Christ or enter into any part of the universe, including earth since the earth then will be the new earth without the presence of any kind of evil whatsoever. It amounts to the end of the immortal state they were in after their physical death and the final judgment.

7. When Jesus said, "Fear only Him who can destroy both your soul and body in hell" (Matthew 10:28), it indicates at some point of time the souls which are ungodly will face torment in hell and final destruction or annihilation in the Lake of Fire. We find that the death and hell together are going to be thrown into the Lake of Fire. Death and hell shall be no more. God does not do anything without a purpose.
8. The one who is the sovereign God and has the power to create has the power to destroy also. God has the power to bring immortality to an end because there is no purpose to keep them under torment and suffering forever and ever. God is holy and righteous.

"Blessed and holy is he that part in the first resurrection: on such the second death has no power" (Revelation 20:6). It is appointed unto men once to die and after this the judgment (Hebrews 9:27). When God has ordained for men once to die, where is the question of second death? In the final judgment, only one thing matters—whether you are godly or ungodly. There is nothing in between. All those who are godly get to inherit the kingdom of God. All those who are ungodly will be thrown into hell and later in to the Lake of Fire and extinguished. They shall be seen or found no more, no need, and no return. That is what second death means!

What Is Eternal (Everlasting) Fire?

Fire is eternal from God's perspective. It was there from the beginning, and it is going to be there forever under God's control. That is why it is designated as eternal fire. The fire will be there eternally unless God wants to do away with it. Fire throughout the Bible was used by God for so many different purposes. He Himself dwells in the midst of fire. There is fire in heaven too, and that fire has to be eternal. In many occasions, we find in the Bible that the fire came down from heaven.

1. God (the Angel of the Lord) appeared to Moses in a flame of fire from the midst of a bush. So, he looked, and behold, the bush was burning with fire, but the bush was not consumed. (Exodus 3:2)
2. The Lord descended upon Mount Sinai in *fire*. Here we see it was like a furnace and the whole mount quaked greatly (Exodus 19:18).
3. The sight of the glory of the Lord was like *devouring fire* on the top of the mountain in the eyes of the children of Israel (Exodus 24:27).
4. God went before the Israelites in *fire* to lead them during the night (Exodus 14:21).
5. God has the power over the fire to prevent it from consuming anything, including men. He appeared to Moses in the burning bush; the bush was not burnt (Exodus 3:2). In Daniel 3:20–25, we read that Shadrach, Meshach, and Abednego were thrown in to the burning fiery furnace, but the flame of the fire slew those men who carried them to the furnace, but these men were seen walking in the midst of the fire! What a contrast! Clearly it indicates that God has the power over fire and no one else, including Satan and his associates.
6. God has made His ministers a *flaming fire* and not a flame of fire (Psalm 104:4). It is very often misunderstood as a flame of fire, which could be quenched by some means. Flaming fire denotes the authority the ministers of the gospel have over all the works of the devil.
7. The Holy Spirit appeared as cloven tongues like as of fire and rested upon each of them who were gathered in the Upper Room (Acts 2:3).
8. God caused the *fire* to fall down on the altar that Elijah has prepared for making the sacrifice. This altar was made by stones. In 1 Kings 18:38, we read that the fire of the Lord fell and *consumed* the burnt sacrifice, the wood, *stones*, and even the dust, and licked up the water that was in the trench. The fire from God could consume even the *stones*,

in this case to prove this is how it is going to be in the final destruction.
9. God sent fire from heaven to destroy the 102 men the king of Samaria had sent to meet the man of God, Elijah, and mocked the God of Israel. Elijah spoke the words of God, and the fire fell down and consumed them (2 Kings 1:9–14).
10. God has an army with chariots of fire. We read in 2 Kings 2:11, Elijah was taken up into heaven in chariots of fire, and in 2:17, we read God has provided an army of chariots of fire around the Prophet Elisha (2 Kings 6:17).
11. Above all, God is a *consuming fire* (Deuteronomy 4:24, Hebrews 12:29).

Sun is a ball of fire, and so the stars. Fire was used by God for many good purposes, as well as for the purpose of destruction. He is also designated as consuming fire. He used the pillar of fire to protect the Israelites by night. He consumes the sacrifices by sending the fire from above. He has consumed even people alive by sending fire on them. He is using fire to protect people also. So what we have to understand here is the *fire is always eternal* and *everlasting* since the beginning. And it stays eternal. God is using the fire, which is eternally existent whenever and wherever He wants to use it and how! But the purpose for which God is using the fire has to be properly understood.

Eternal Fire Used for Judgment and Total Extinction

The use of the eternal fire for judgment and total extinction is seen in many references in the Scriptures. Let us read carefully the following passage from Deuteronomy 29:22–29. In verse 23, we read that the land of Sodom and Gomorrah and Admah and Zeboim, which the Lord overthrew in His anger and in His wrath, burnt out to the extent that nothing could ever be sown. It could not bear anything, and any grass would never be grown there. Then the nations will say, "Wherefore has the Lord done this unto this land, what meanest the heat of His great anger?" Verse 29 reads that the Lord rooted them out in *anger* and *great indignation*.

When Jude refers this incident he writes: "Even as Sodom and Gomorrah and the about them in like manner, giving themselves over to fornication, and going after strange flesh, are set forth *for an example*, suffering the *vengeance of eternal fire*" (Jude 7). We see here the phrase *eternal fire* is used clearly indicating that fire is eternally existent, and hence, it is called as *eternal fire*. But it does not mean it will be burning forever and ever. We don't see Sodom and Gomorrah still burning, although we read it suffered the vengeance of eternal fire. We also read in Jude 13, "Twice dead plucked up by the roots; raging waves of the sea, foaming out of their own shame; wandering stars, to whom it is reserved the *blackness* of *darkness* forever." Could it mean the *second death* and *total extinction*?

Let us consider what Peter wrote about this: "For if God spared not the angels that sinned, but cast the down to hell [Tartarus in Greek, a dark place of punishment], and delivered them into chains of darkness, to be reserved unto judgment; and spares not the old world, but saved Noah the eighth person, a preacher of righteousness, bringing in the flood upon the world of the ungodly; and turning the cities of Sodom and Gomorrah into ashes, condemned them to extinction, making them an example to those who were to be ungodly. For the Lord knows how to deliver godly out of temptations, and to reserve the ungodly unto the Day of Judgment to be punished" (2 Peter 2:4–9).

How clearly Peter exposes the mind and plan of God. Everyone who is godly will be *protected* and *justified*. Everyone who is *ungodly* will be punished and then extinguished. All those who have rebelled against God, including the angels, are undergoing sufferings of some kind in the place of darkness and are kept for the day of judgment. This judgment is the *final white throne judgment* by Jesus Christ. After the judgment, the ungodly will be sentenced for the final extinction in the Lake of Fire. We find in Revelation 20:14 that the *death*, which is an inanimate matter, and the hell (Hades), which was holding all the ungodly since the time creation, whether angels or humans together, will be cast into the Lake of Fire, which is the *second death*. That is the final fate of all the rebellious and ungodly creatures. They will be totally extinguished, and they will *be no more.*

CHAPTER 16

The Black Hole (Source: Wikipedia)

A black hole is a place in space where gravity pulls so much that even light cannot get out. The gravity is so strong because matter has been squeezed into a tiny space. This can happen when a star is dying. Because no light can get out, people can't see black holes. They are invisible. This is the scientific discovery. They were so far able to identify nearly ten such holes in our Milky Way so far, where our solar system is located. In the similar manner, the sun also could become a black hole sometime soon. Maybe after the millennium, which means after one thousand years or even later, the sun will become a black hole.

The blackness of darkness referred by Apostle Jude in the book of Jude chapter 13 takes us to the existence of black hole in every galaxy in the universe, including the galaxy in which our solar system is found. Revelation 21:1 reads, "The first heaven and the first earth were passed away, and there was no more sea." When we read it together with Jude 13, the raging waves of the sea, foaming out of their own shame; wandering stars, to whom is reserved the blackness of darkness, the old heaven and old earth could possibly be sucked in to the black hole in our galaxy when the sun becomes the black hole, and neither the sun nor the earth will return again. Nobody could see the inside of the black hole as the scientists have declared because of the tremendous gravitational force exhibited by it. Even the light will be sucked in, and it will not be able the drive away the darkness as we normally see and know.

This is also confirmed by Jesus when He prophesied about the end-time happenings: "Immediately of those days the Sun be darkened [will become a black hole], and because there is no light from the Sun, the moon shall not give her light and the stars shall fall from heaven and the powers of the heaven shall be shaken" (Matthew 24:29). Jesus foretold that the sun will become a black hole. The scientists also have confirmed that when the sun becomes a black hole, it will suck at least three planets from the solar system, including the earth, which explains that the old earth shall pass away along with its contents, namely the Lake of Fire, which is now containing the death and hell. So the death and hell shall be no more and never to be seen anymore. What will happen to that after it is being sucked into the black hole, there is nothing said in the Bible. All that we know is there is no return for the old earth. A new earth will appear, and all those who are with Christ shall live forever and ever with Him.

A *black hole* is a region of space-time exhibiting such strong gravitational effects that *nothing*—not even particles and electromagnetic radiation such as light—can escape from inside it. The theory of general relativity predicts that a sufficiently compact mass (like the sun) can deform space-time to form a black hole. The boundary of the region from which no escape is possible is called the event horizon. Although crossing the event horizon has enormous effect on the fate of the object crossing it, it appears to have no locally detectable features. In many ways, a black hole acts like an ideal black body as it reflects no light. Moreover, quantum field theory in curved space-time predicts that even horizons emit Hawking radiation, with the same spectrum as a black body of a temperature inversely proportional to its mass. This temperature is on the order of billionths of a Kelvin for black holes of stellar mass, making it essentially impossible to observe.

Objects whose gravitational fields are too strong for light to escape were first considered in the eighteenth century by John Michel and Pierre-Simon Laplace. The first modern solution of general relativity that would characterize a black hole was found by

Karl Schwarzschild in 1916, although its interpretation as a region of space from which nothing can escape was first published by David Finkelstein in 1958. Black holes were long considered a mathematical curiosity; it was during the 1960s that theoretical work showed they were a generic prediction of general relativity. The discovery of neutron stars sparked interest in gravitationally collapsed compact objects as a possible astrophysical reality.

Black holes of stellar mass are expected to form when very massive stars collapse at the end of their life cycle. After a black hole has formed, it can continue to grow by absorbing mass from its surroundings. By absorbing other stars and merging with other black holes, super massive black holes of millions of solar masses may form. There is general consensus that super massive black holes exist in the centers of most galaxies (including our galaxy). Despite its invisible interior, the presence of a black hole can be inferred through its interaction with other matter and with electromagnetic radiation, such as visible light. Matter that falls onto a black hole can form an external accretion disk heated by friction. In this way, astronomers have identified numerous stellar black hole candidates in binary systems and established that the radio source known as Sagittarius A at the core of our own Milky Way galaxy contains a super massive black hole of about 4.3 million masses. The Scripture says the death will be no more (Revelation 21:4), sickness will be no more, curse will be no more, Satan will be no more, and the second heaven (midair, which Satan and his associates are occupying) will be no more. This earth (old earth and this world system) will be no more, hell will be no more, and everything is going to be new. He who sat on the throne said, "Behold, I make all things new, write, for these words are true and faithful" (Revelation 21:1–5).

On February 11, 2016, the LIGO collaboration announced the first observation of gravitational waves. Because these waves were generated from a black hole merger, it was the first-ever direct detection of a binary black hole merger. On June 15, 2016, a second detection of a gravitational wave event from colliding black holes was announced.

When we consider the purpose of eternal punishment, it gives us an indication that there is no purpose. God does not do anything without a purpose. After the final judgement, the act of casting Satan and all those who are with him into the hell and later into the lake of fire clearly indicates to us that there is going to be no return for them. Moreover, the old earth is going to be sucked into the sun black hole into total darkness. Nobody, not even anyone in heaven, is going to be concerned or worried about what is going to be the future for them. Some say that it is going to be a monument to remember for all eternity that they are suffering like this because of what they did to Christ. I have no opinion to comment on this. Let God be the judge. We don't want to remember him, neither want to see him anymore nor suffer under him anymore. We would rather forget the whole thing and spend the eternity happily with our Lord Jesus Christ. Hallelujah! Amen.

So the second death is going to be the end of the old and the beginning of the new. Hallelujah!

CHAPTER 17

God's Intelligent Design for the Eternal Future

Theologians and scientists were arguing and debating over the origin of the universe and man, creation or evolution, and they are still not able to come to any concrete understanding or conclusion. They don't seem to be worried about the future at all. I am of the opinion that let the scientists worry about the past and let the theologians worry about the future. As much as the Scripture gives details about the past and the present, it also gives more details and more importance about the future. Jesus Christ has spent most of His time teaching about the future eternity. I fail to understand why the so-called Christian leaders, true Christians, and Bible scholars talk very little about the future. I do understand that the life in this world is important. To live happy, healthy, comfortable, and long enough are definitely to be taken care of. Focusing our attention more and more to these things takes us away from any thought about the eternity. Jesus's one saying explains it all. Jesus said to His disciples, "Whosoever will try himself to save his life, he shall lose it; whosoever will lose his life for My sake shall find it. What is a man profited if he shall gain the whole world and lose his own soul? Or what shall a man give in exchange for his soul?" (Matthew 16:25–26) This is the core of His teachings, and this is for which He came and died on the cross of Calvary.

WHO RULES THE WORLD, GOD OR SATAN?

After long debates and arguments, evolution theory is losing support from both scientists and atheists day by day as number of unanswered questions keep rising in the evolution theory. Creationists, after much debate, have come to a conclusion that "intelligent design" has to be basis for the existence of the universe and man with many unanswered question of the origin of life. The study of intelligent design should be introduced into schools; this was a proposal supported by then President Bush in 2005. But unfortunately, it received both support and criticisms from the members of the Congress. Whatever it is, the majority of the scientists have agreed that the intelligent design is lot more dependable to prove the creation theory, and there should be a designer who could be the invisible person otherwise designated as God.

However, for true Christian believers, this is just an additional support to believe in the Creator more and more. Now this sovereign God, who is the creator and the ruler of the entire universe, has the power to destroy all those matters and lives which He thinks need not exist anymore. The Scriptures endorse the view that souls can also be destroyed without further existence. "Fear Him who can kill your soul and able to destroy both soul and body in hell" (Matthew 10:28). You can bring up many arguments like "Soul is immortal," "It never dies," "It will live for ever and ever," "Soul will live for all eternity." The simple question is "What is the purpose?" All ungodly wicked souls which are finally going to end up in hell and later the hell and the death together is going to be thrown into the Lake of Fire. For what? To keep burning forever and ever? Who is going to keep watching it? Hell, death, and Satan with all his followers are also going to end up in the Lake of Fire. Are they going to have a second chance maybe after a million years to come to normal life, accept and obey Jesus's kingship, and be a goody-goody guy? No way! Then why should they exist anymore even in the burning hell?

Then why should it last for ever and ever? Just think! God has brought in a number of changes in the life of human beings.

1. First He created man with no prescribed life span.

2. Then sin and death came in, and his life span was around nine hundred years.
3. Then slowly God reduced his life span step by step to 300 years, to 150 years, then to 100 years, and now fixed it between 70 and 100 years.
4. Now when you believe in Jesus, you get your eternal life back again.
5. It is immaterial at what age you physically die.
6. Soul and spirit do not die; it becomes immortal, wait until the day of judgment, and then enter into eternity and will live with Jesus forever and ever.
7. Wicked souls and spirits also become immortal until they appear before the judgment seat of Jesus Christ. Once the judgment is given, they are all going to be thrown in to hell, and later the Lake of Fire, which is the second death. After the second death, which is equal to total extinction, where is question of eternity for such souls and spirits?
8. God, who created the souls, can destroy them too! Everything which were created is subjected to destruction. It is purely his discretion and decision.
9. God need not keep hell as a monument as some people claim and teach!
10. Old heaven and old earth together with hell shall pass away, and no will be able to identify them anymore! For sure, God does not want to keep Satan anymore.

New Heaven and New Earth

Finally, the old heaven (the second heaven which is being occupied by Satan and his associates) and the old earth (the cursed earth because of Adam's Sin) are going to pass away, and new heaven and new earth are going to be ushered in to be ruled by Jesus Himself (Revelation 21:1). So the entire rebellious, ungodly, cursed heaven and earth are going to be destroyed (annihilated) without any trace because new heaven and new earth are going to be ushered in. Scriptures tell us that the first heaven and the first earth were passed away, and there was no more sea. Theologians argue that "pass away" means pass from one condition to the other.

"And I [John] saw a new heaven and a new earth. For the first heaven [referring to the heaven occupied by Satan and his spirits] and the first earth [referring to the earth occupied by mankind] were passed away, and there was no more sea." This clearly indicates that only this earth was created for the livelihood of mankind, and other forms of living things since water is required for life to exist. As far as the scientific knowledge goes, there is no sea or water found in any other planet in the solar system or elsewhere in the other systems or galaxies. The argument of "looking for the traces of water or the presence of any kind of sea" is just an assumption and inappropriate hope to divert the attention of mankind away from the existence of God.

Right now, there is a city in heaven called Jerusalem, also referred to as the holy city in the third heaven, which is the dwelling place of God and also the tabernacle of God. The ancient city of Jerusalem in heaven was governed by the king and priest Melchizedek, who by interpretation was called the King of Righteousness and the King of Peace (King of Salem which means "peace") as a type of Jesus Christ. As much as his genealogy could not be traced (he was without father, without mother, and without descent, having neither beginning of days nor end of life), he was made like unto the Son of God, Jesus Christ (Hebrews 7:1–3). Hence, the original holy city of God called the heavenly Jerusalem was governed by Melchizedek, which is going to descend in the form of new earth from heaven. The king and the high priest of this New Jerusalem is going to be Jesus Christ Himself, who is going to rule this new city in righteousness and peace.

In Revelation 22:1–5, John is now describing how the government in the new earth is going to be. The New Jerusalem will descend from the heavens. If you want to visualize with scientific eyes, you may not be able to comprehend it. For those who do not believe in the creation of the universe and mankind, it will be hard to visualize how the New Jerusalem is going to come down from the heavens. The creation is a fact because we are all generations of God-created human beings. What the Scripture describes about the new heavens and the new earth is going to take place. For those who do not want to believe, let that be a secret till they see them. For those who believe, it is a sweet expectation.

The Scriptures read, "John saw a pure river of water of life, clear as crystal, proceeding out of the throne of God and of the Lamb. In the midst of the streets of it, on either side of the river, there was the tree of life [which was protected and removed from the Garden of Eden]. These trees bare twelve manner of fruits yielding every month, and the leaves of the trees were for the healing of the Nations" (Revelation 22:1–2).

"There will be no more curse: but the Throne of God and of the Lamb shall be in it; and His servants shall serve Him. They shall see His face and HIS name shall be in their foreheads. There shall be [no need be] no light there. They don't need a candle, neither the light of the Sun. The Lord give them light: and they shall reign for ever and ever" (Revelation 22:3–5). There is no need for an enormous research on this. For those people who keep asking how it is possible, my contention for such people would be, let them keep doing the research forever. They will keep doing it as long as Satan instigate them until he is removed from the earth.

Many theologians and Bible scholars have the opinion that there is no New Jerusalem coming out of heaven, but only this earth is going to be recreated or replenished or cleaned up with no curse and no Satan, who is the root cause of all sin and curse. The Bible does not endorse this view whatsoever. You will find the full explanation why that is not going to happen in the next section.

New Earth Will Be Totally Righteous

According to His promise, we look for new heavens and a new earth, where in dwells righteousness (2 Peter 3:13). For many, it is hard to understand and believe. For them, it just means a renovated earth. I don't know whether they think it is going to be hard for God to create another new earth. He can create as many earths as He wants. I have no problem in believing it. I also want to explain that God is not going to be stuck with this totally cursed old earth. In the medical field, when we want any matter or material that has been very badly infected with a highly infective and seriously contagious organisms, like bacteria or virus, we go through a process called incineration. This is a process by which we get rid of those infective organisms, like bacteria or virus, whatever it may be, at a very high temperature in which nothing but ashes will be left over. It is equal to annihilation. They will never exist anymore. We have a Lake of Fire right under our feet at a temperature of over six thousand degrees Celsius, and we are expecting something will survive that temperature forever and ever. This looks unbelievable to me even from the scientific point of view. The second death will be something like that.

In Isaiah 65:17, we read thus: "Behold I create new heavens and a new earth. The former [the heaven and earth we are living in right now] shall not be remembered, nor come in to mind." God says he is going to create a new earth. Where is the question of renovating, replenishing, or recreating? Are we more intelligent than God? The old earth is gone and to be forgotten. Don't even have the slightest thought in your mind about it! If you are good enough to inherit the kingdom of God, just go and enjoy the new heaven and the new earth.

"There shall be counting days for our life. A child shall life for one hundred years. They shall build houses and inhabit them. They shall plant vineyards and eat the fruits of them. Their days will be as long a tree lives. They will enjoy the works of their hands. They shall not labor in vain. Nobody will bring forth any trouble. A total trouble free environment. Even before we call God will answer! And while they are yet speaking God shall hear. The wolf and the lamb will feed together. The lion shall eat straw like bullock. They shall not hurt nor destroy in all my holy mountain, says the LORD" (Isaiah 65:20–25). This is just imaginary taste of the new heaven and the new earth. There is a lot more to inherit and see.

"'As the New Heavens and New Earth, which I [God] will make, shall remain before me,' said the LORD, 'so shall your seed and your name remain [in to all eternity]'" (Isaiah 66:22). All the occupants of the new earth shall come before the Lord from one new moon to another and from one Sabbath to another forever and ever because the Lord Himself will dwell among them.

John's Vision of New Heaven and New Earth

To understand the full description of the new heaven and new earth, we have to read the entire chapters in Revelation 21 and 22. What the Scriptures tell us is the truth, and all of them are facts to be believed. We have to acknowledge the entire Scriptures are inspired by the Holy Spirit and written by the men of God. None of the prophecies have failed and gone wrong.

Moreover the Scriptures conclude with these words in particular. "Blessed are they that do His commandments that they may have the right to the tree of life, and may enter in through the Gates of the city" (Revelation 22:14).

Further, it also says these words of warning: "I, Jesus, testify unto every man that hearth the words of the prophecy of this book, if any man shall add unto these things, God shall add unto him the plagues that are written in this book; if any man takes away from the words of this book of this prophecy, God will take away his part out of the book of life, and out of the holy city, and from the things which are written in this book" (Revelation 22:18–19).

God has a wonderful and intelligent design for eternity! Hallelujah!

About the Author

The author is basically a veterinarian graduated from Madras Veterinary College, Chennai, Tamil Nadu, India. As a teenager and a student, he found the Lord Jesus Christ as the only savior of the world and wanted to persuade to know more about Him so that he would be able to present Him to the world convincingly. This led him to quit being a veterinarian and take theological studies. He acquired doctorate degrees in theology. This did not stop him from participating in active evangelism. During this period, he had the opportunity to travel around the world a few times, and he gained more and more understanding about the current real situation of the Christians and the churches together in facing the world affairs. He started writing articles on the above subject to many Christian magazines, and finally, he put them all together in the form of this book. The author feels that this is the need of this hour. This is the passion of the author, and he believes that this book will open the understanding of the people and answer many of the unanswered questions about the subject matter of the title. The author is now serving as a pastor of a church and the body of Christ to exhort and edify with the biblical truths.

CPSIA information can be obtained
at www.ICGtesting.com
Printed in the USA
LVHW03s0305231018
594462LV00002B/3/P